AF574358

William Wegman Dogs on Rocks

Edited by Marion Boulton Stroud

Designed by Takaaki Matsumoto, Matsumoto Incorporated

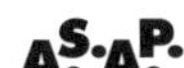

Published by Acadia Summer Arts Program

Published by Acadia Summer Arts Program

Marion Bolton Stroud, Publisher
Takaaki Matsumoto, Matsumoto Incorporated, New York, Producer and Designer
Amy Wilkins, Manager of Publications

Photography by William Wegman

Printed and bound by Nissha Printing Co., Ltd., Kyoto, Japan

Cover image: *A Figure in Hiding*, 2002
Photograph by William Wegman

Library of Congress Control Number: 2008900882
ISBN-13: 978-0-9797642-0-2

Distributed worldwide by D.A.P./Distributed Art Publishers
155 Sixth Avenue, 2nd Floor
New York, New York 10013
Tel: (212) 627.1999
Fax: (212) 627.9484
dap@dapinc.com
www.artbook.com

Batty, Bobbin, Candy, Chip, Chundo, and Penny

The Maine coast provides interesting and challenging locations for me. For the dogs, the buoyant and salty water is unusual. They are used to the freshwater lakes of western Maine, where swimming is more predictable and the water thirst-quenching. On the coast, the land is there and then it is not there. The tide comes in. The fog rolls in. Things wash up. And float away . . . The surprising rocks can be slippery. The sharp stingy things that grow on the rocks can add insult to injury to both dogs and photographer. At times the sky is too bright, the bugs too many.

But sometimes it is just right, every boulder and sea ledge beautiful and accommodating. The pounding surf and omnipresent sea birds exhilarate us and propel the quest.

Photographing the dogs outside is a little like fishing: Find a promising stretch, make a cast, catch and release, move on. Surprisingly, the dogs seem to find the "good spot" for me. In between shots they hunt relentlessly, relenting only as I read the light, guide the pose, and frame and take the shot.

The collection of photographs in this book spans a period of ten years, and includes six dogs from four generations: Chundo, Batty, Chip, Bobbin, Candy, and Penny. Most were taken on Baker's Island, on the Wellington dock in Southwest Harbor, and in a few other places nearby during late July and August.

I am deeply indebted to Kippy Stroud. Without her instigation and unabated encouragement, these pictures would certainly never have been taken. Thank you also to our friends and colleagues at A.S.A.P. (dogs and humans alike) for putting up with our Weimaraner invasions. And thanks to Rick Savage, captain of the Poor Richard and the Aziscohos, for proving that half the fun is getting there.

William Wegman, 2007

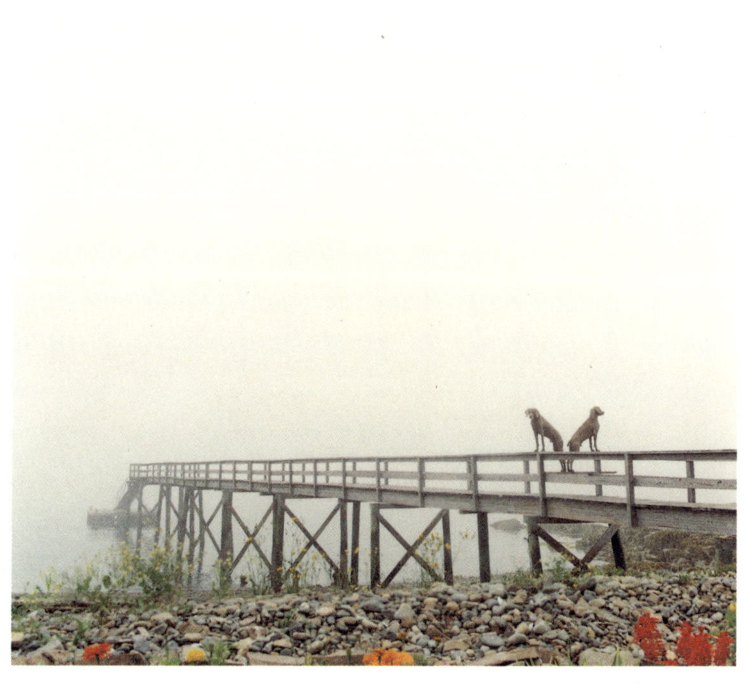

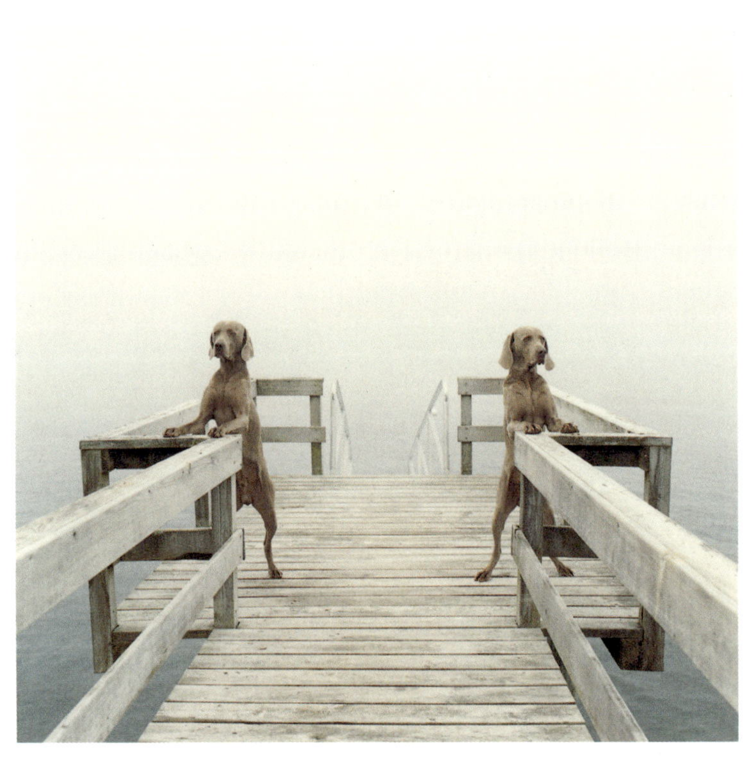

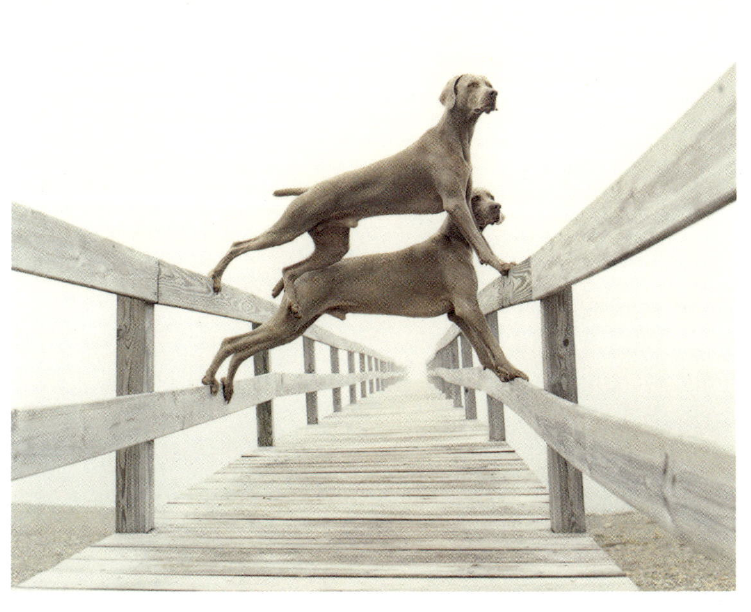

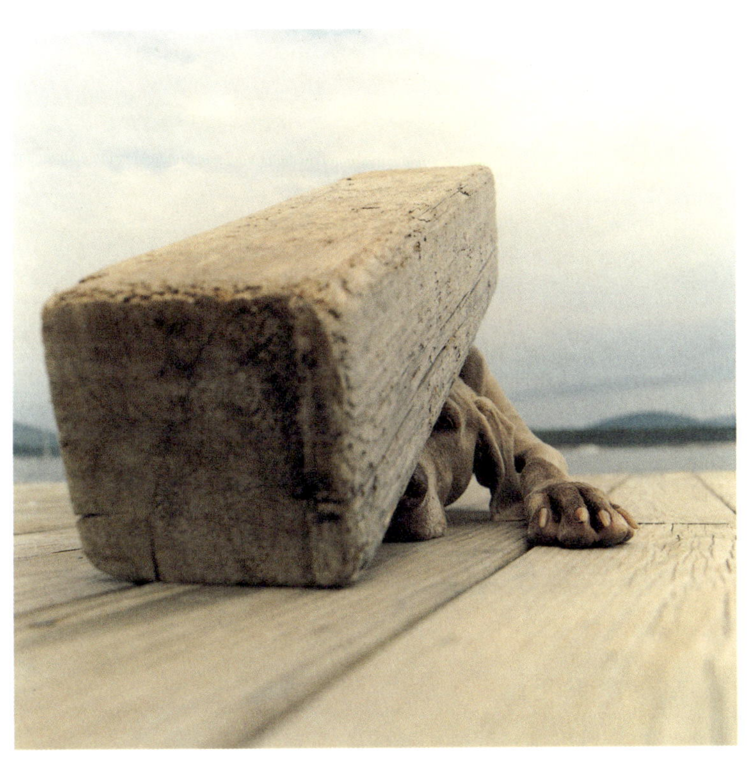

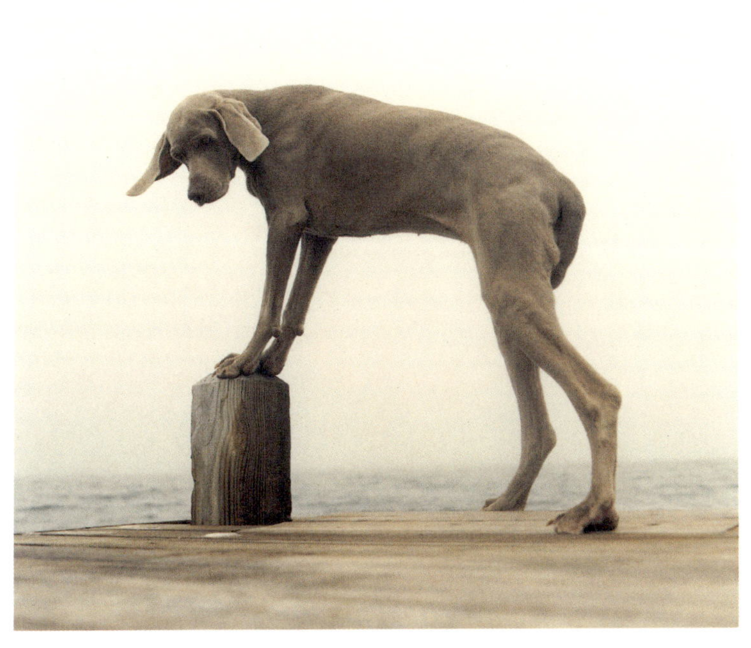

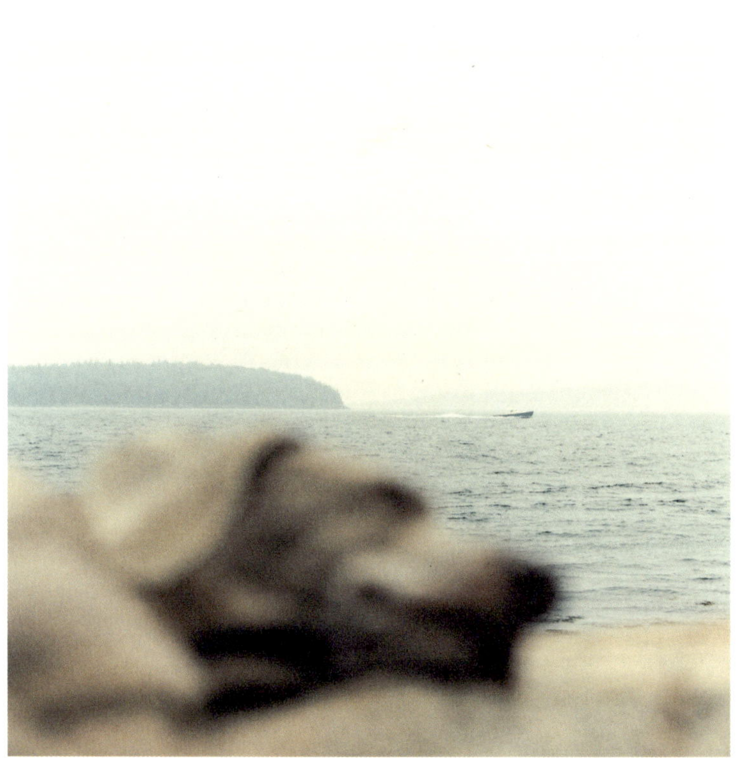

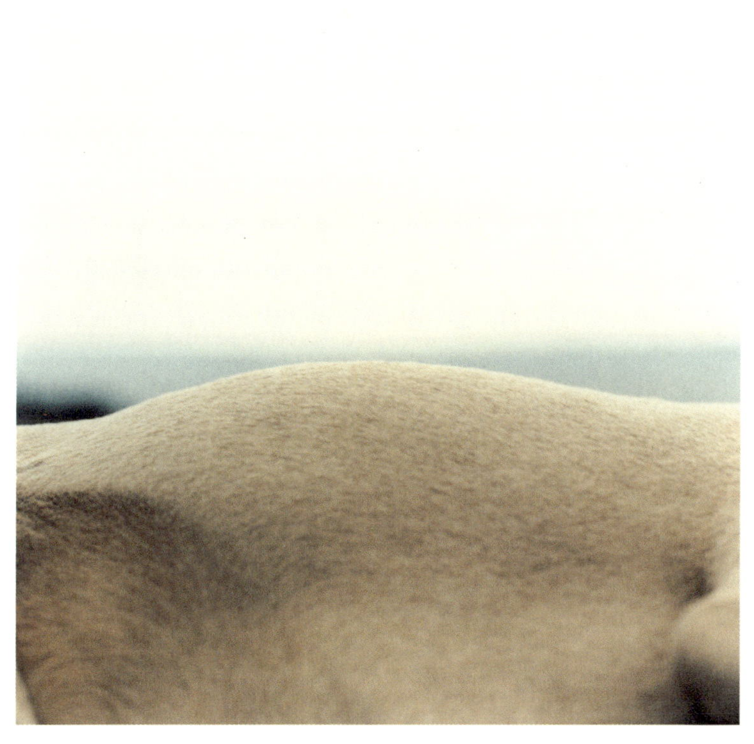

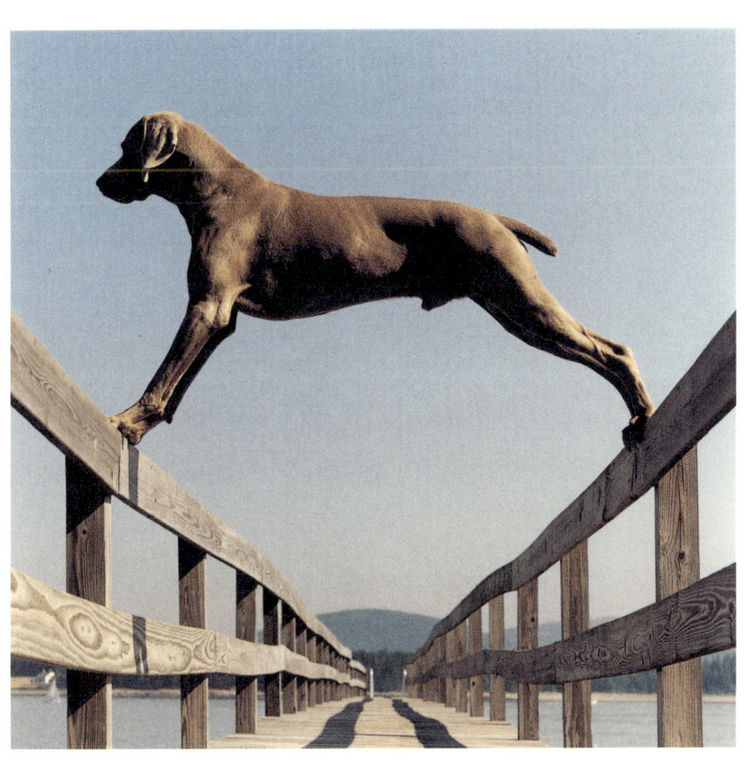

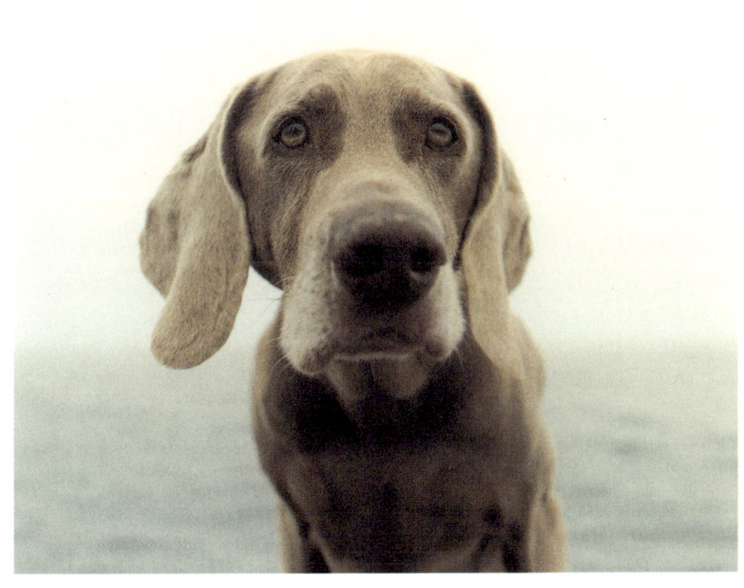

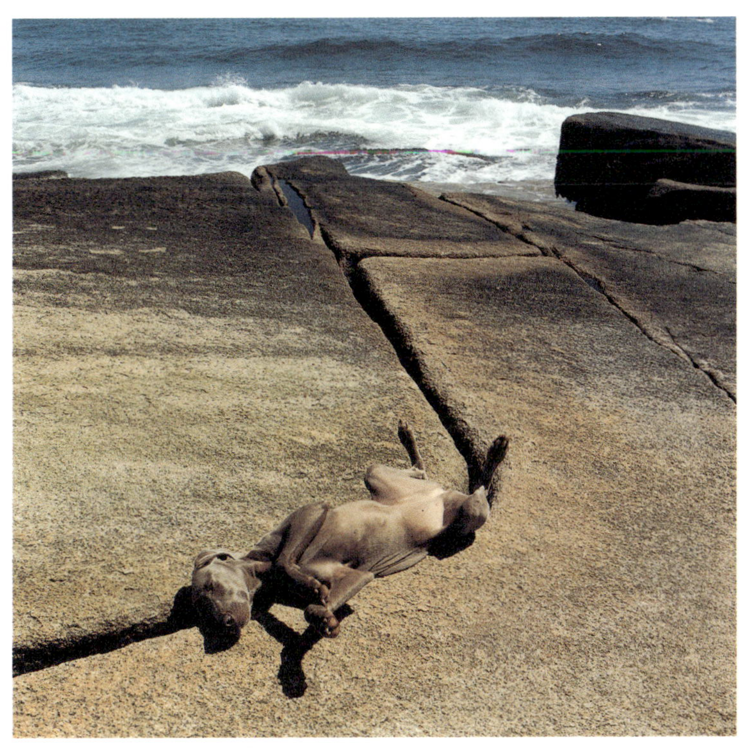

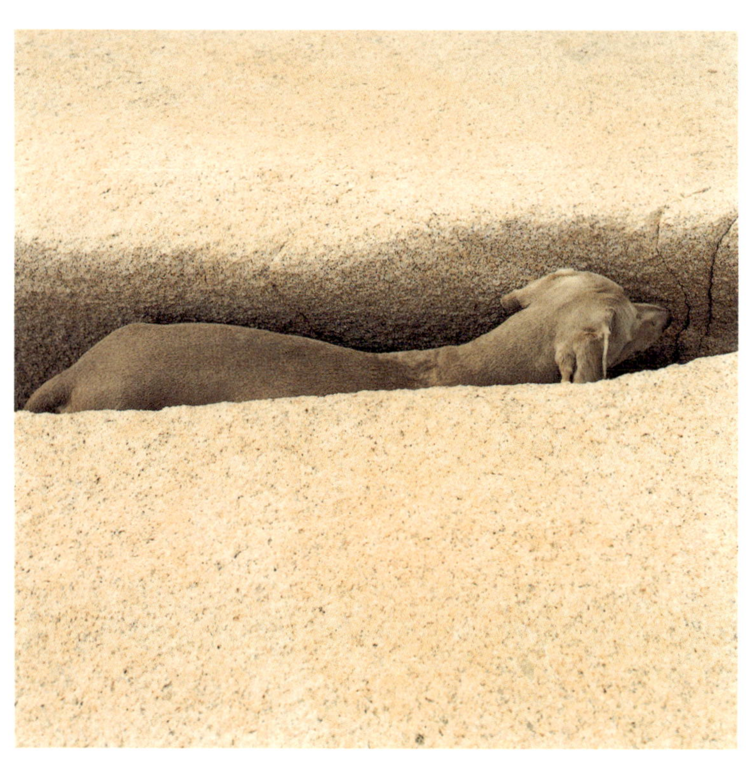

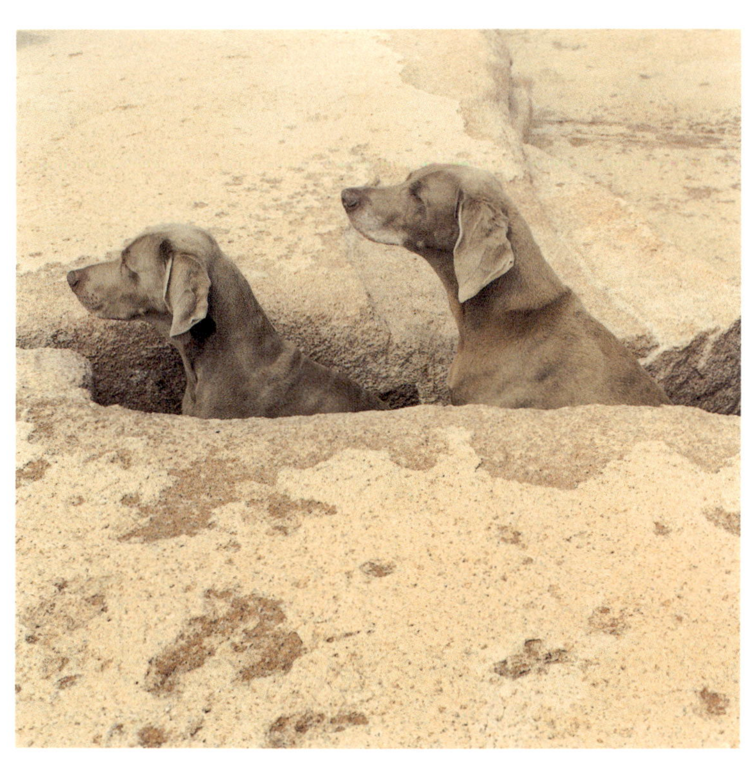

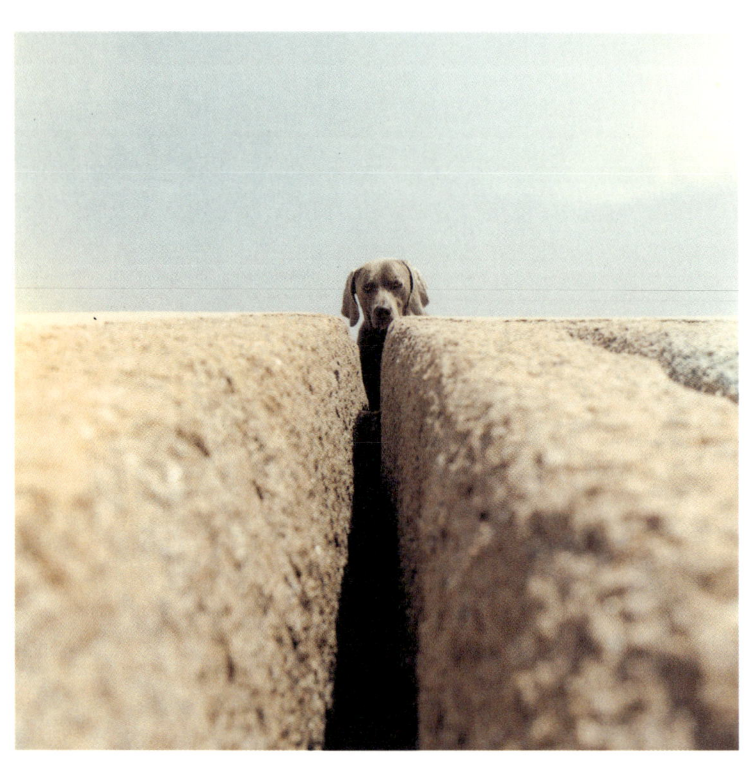

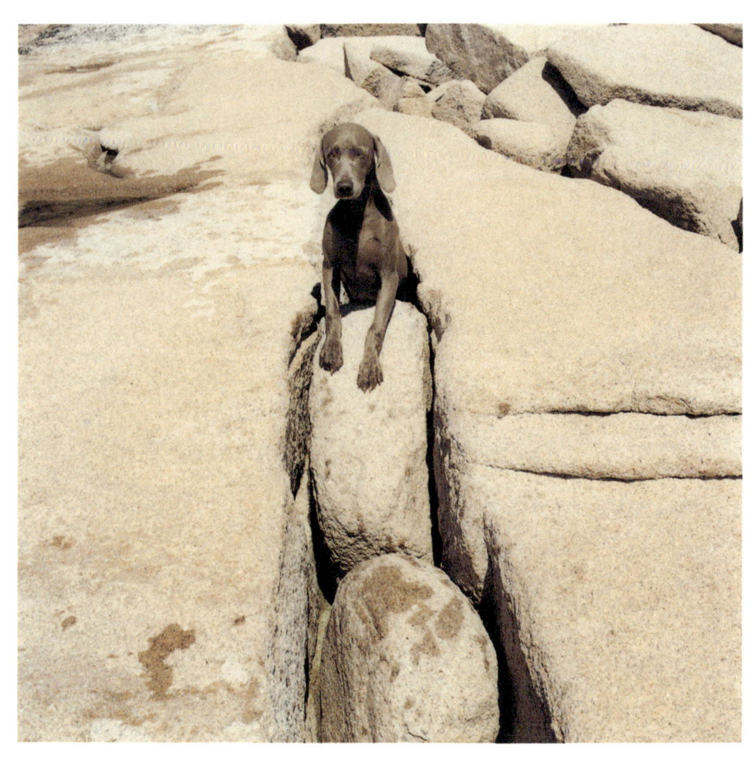

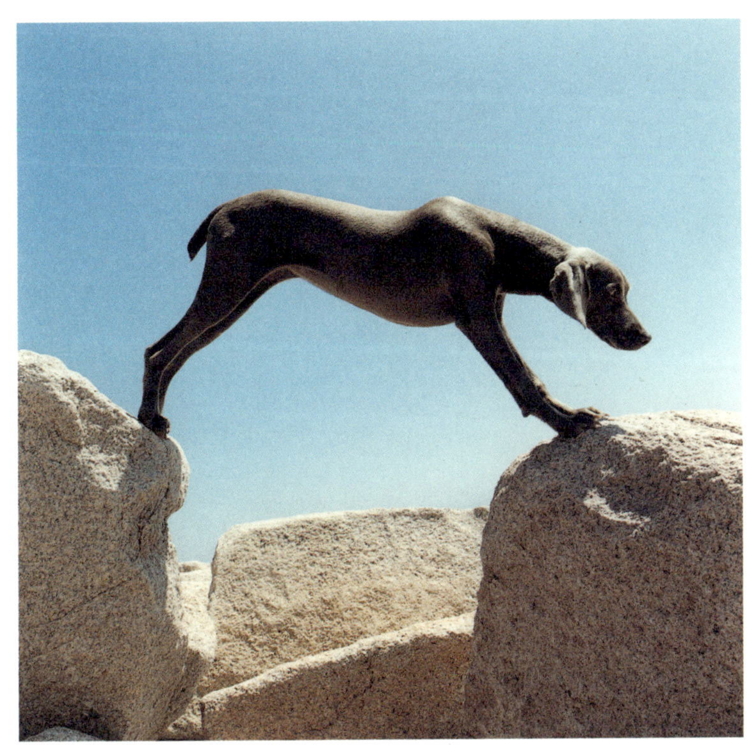

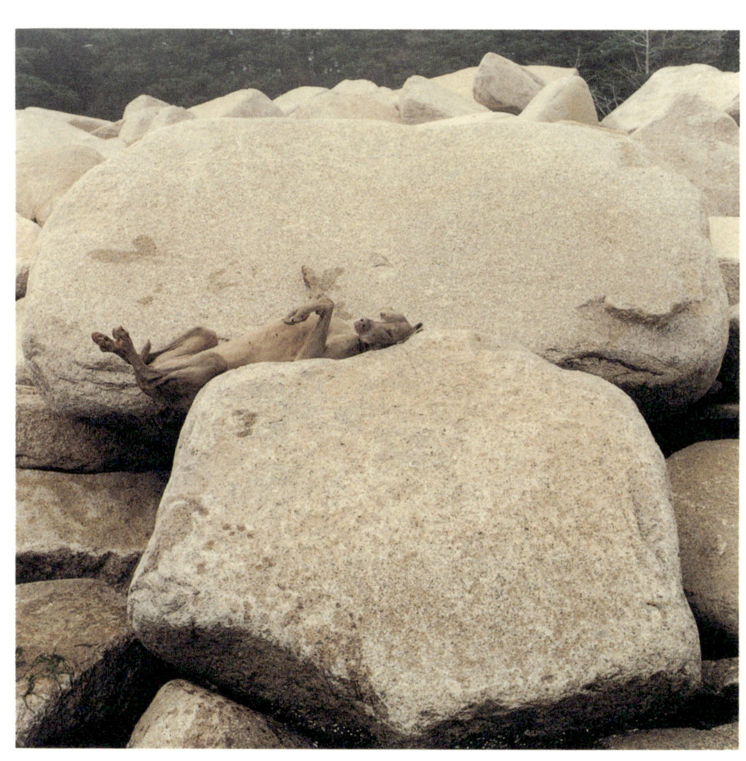

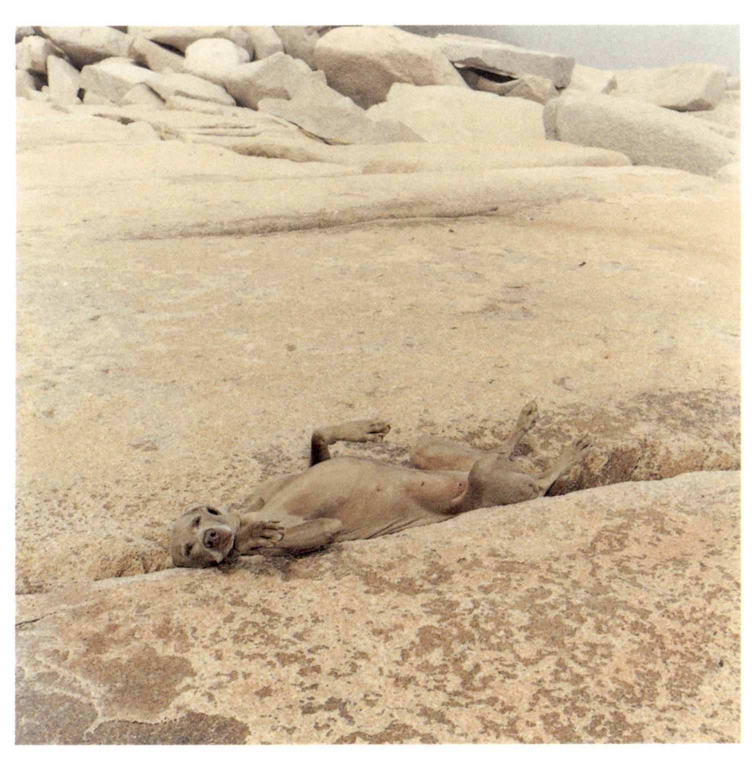

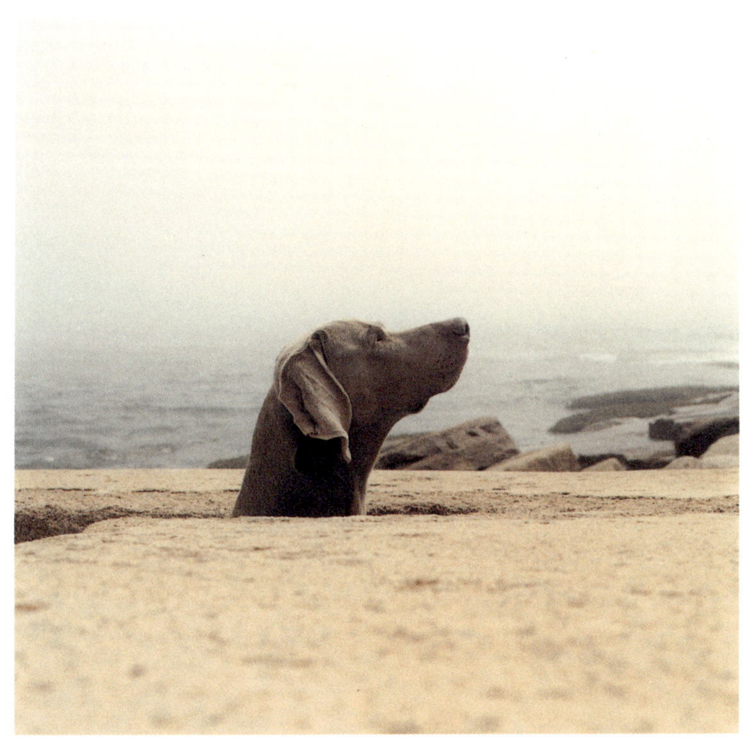

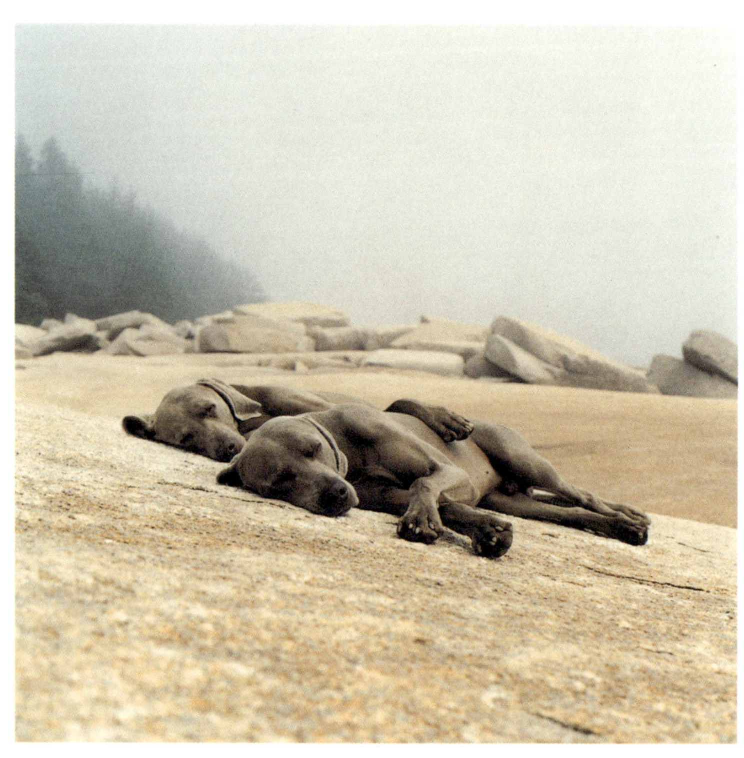

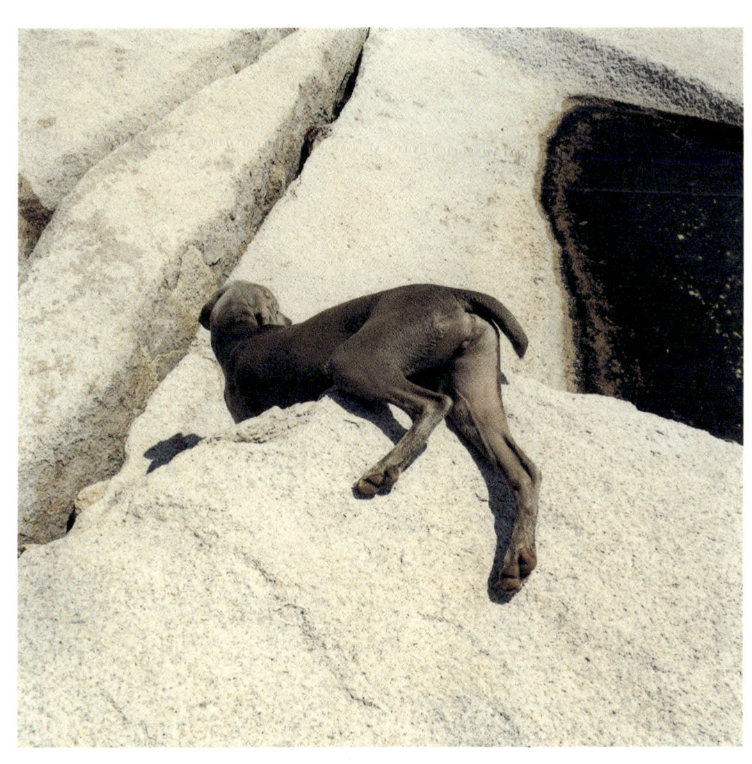

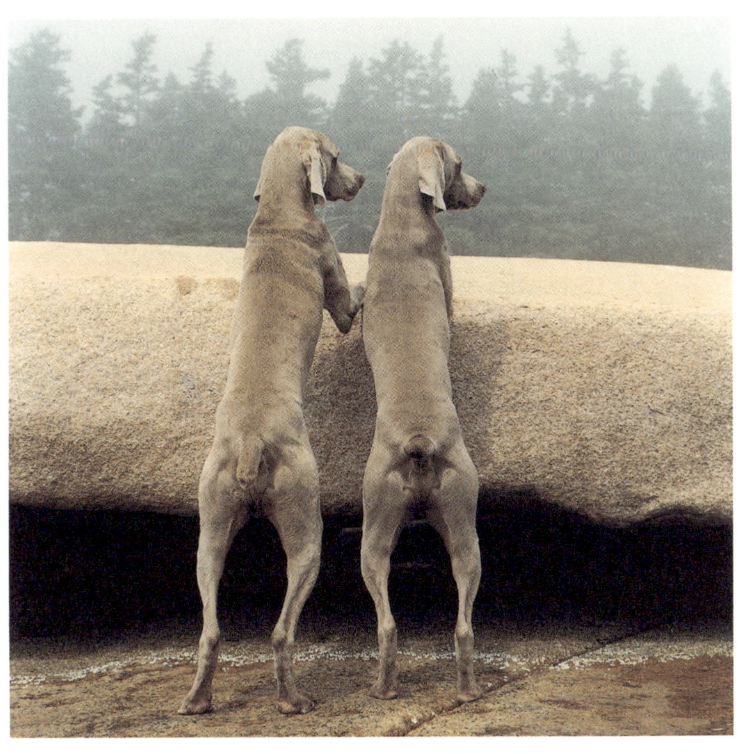

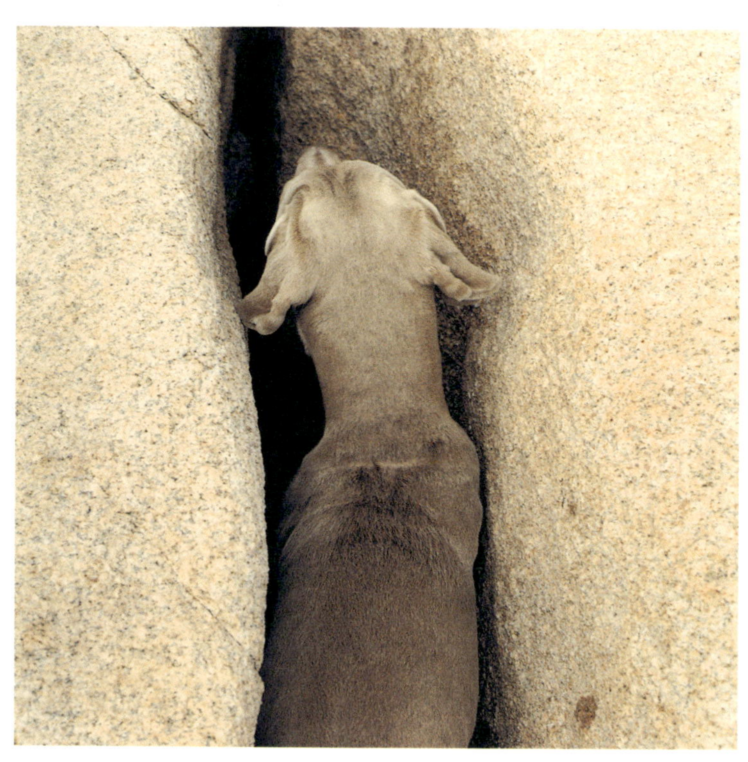

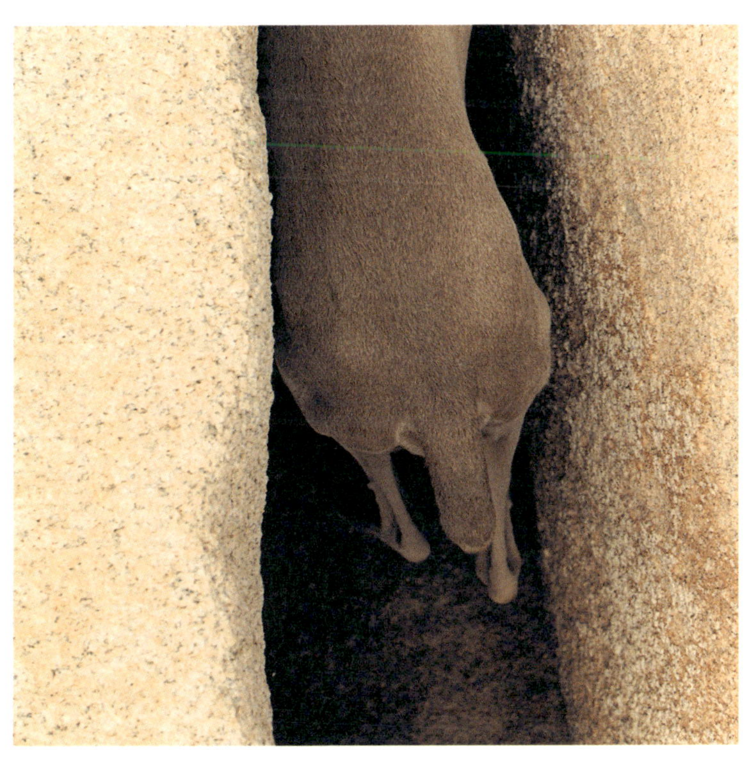

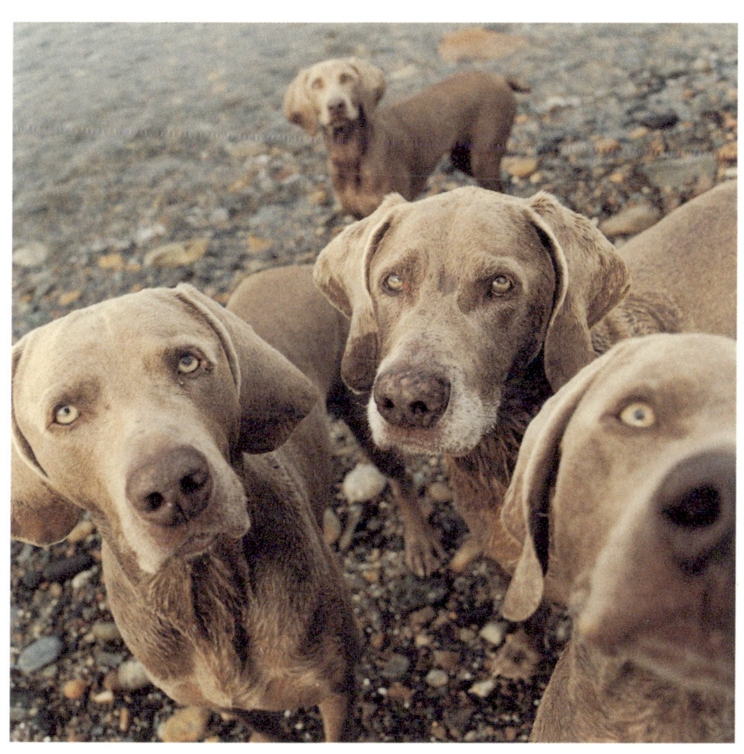

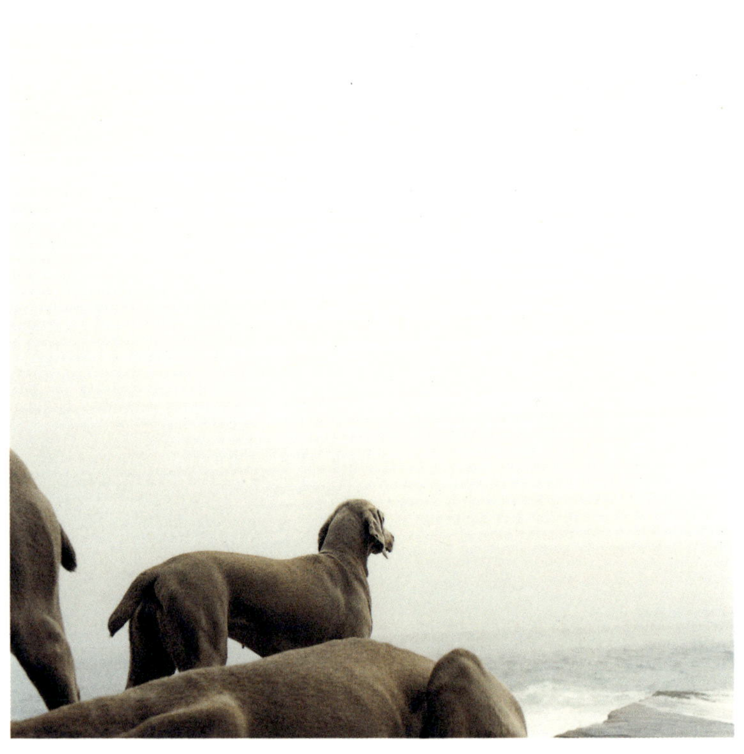

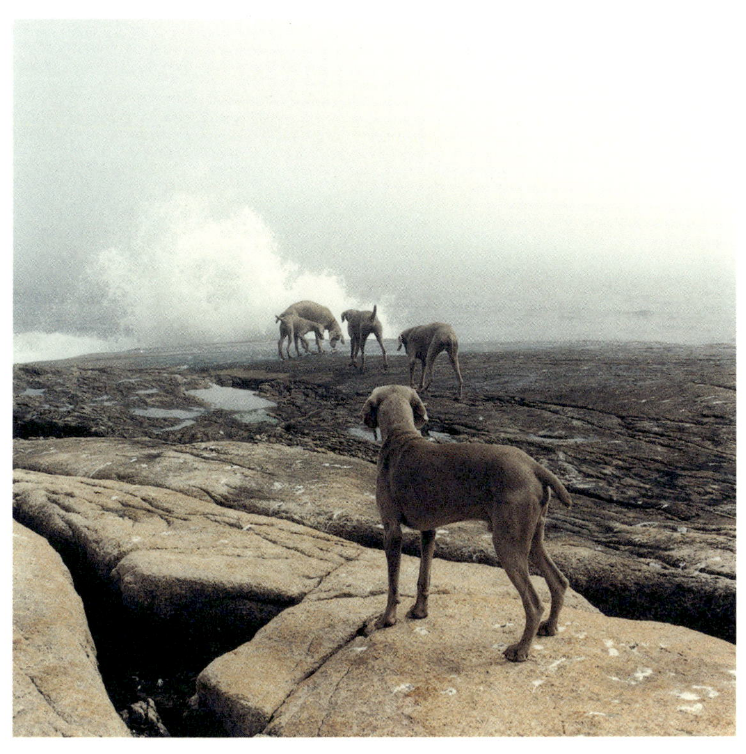

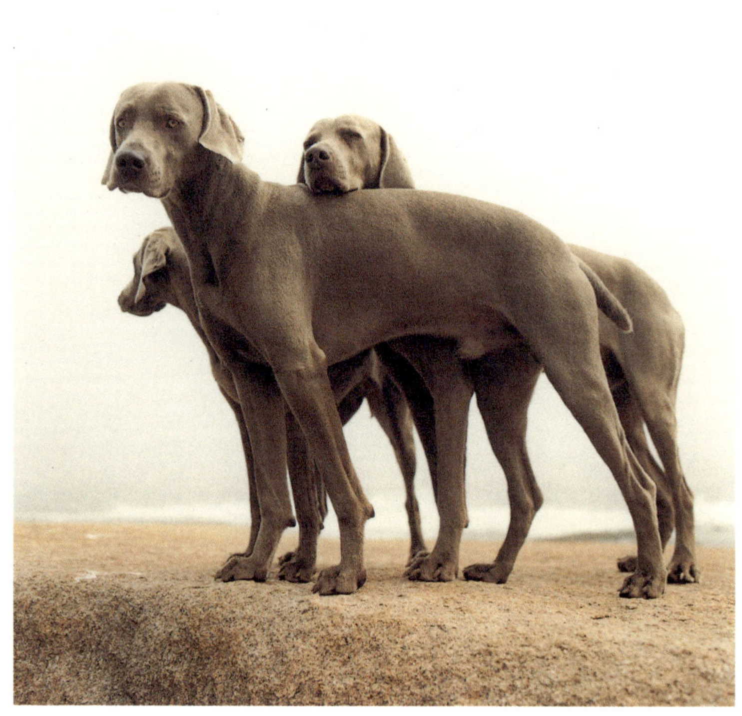

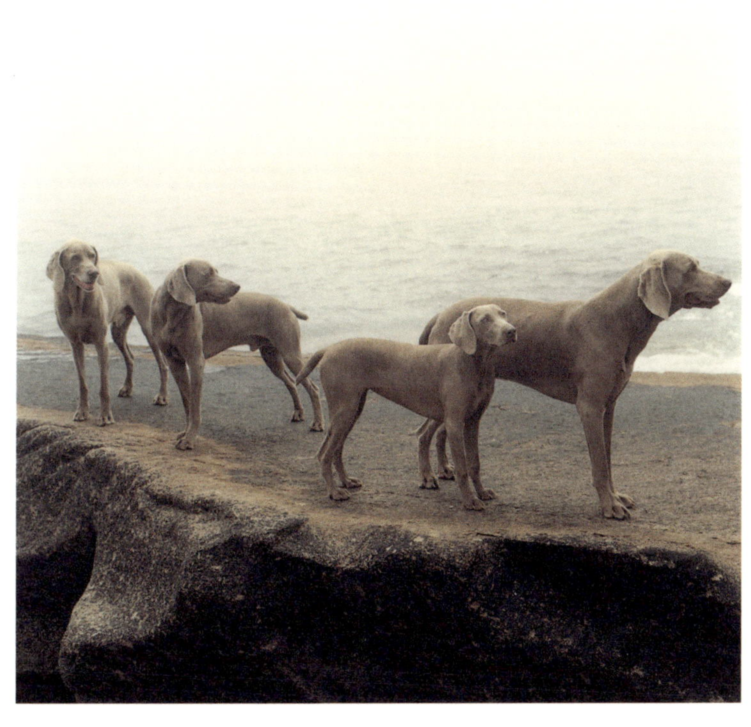

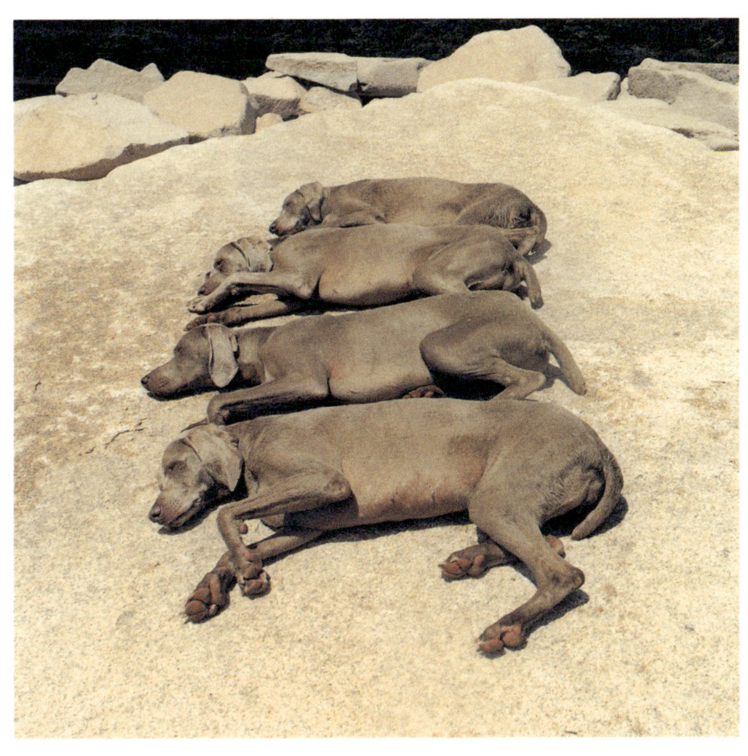

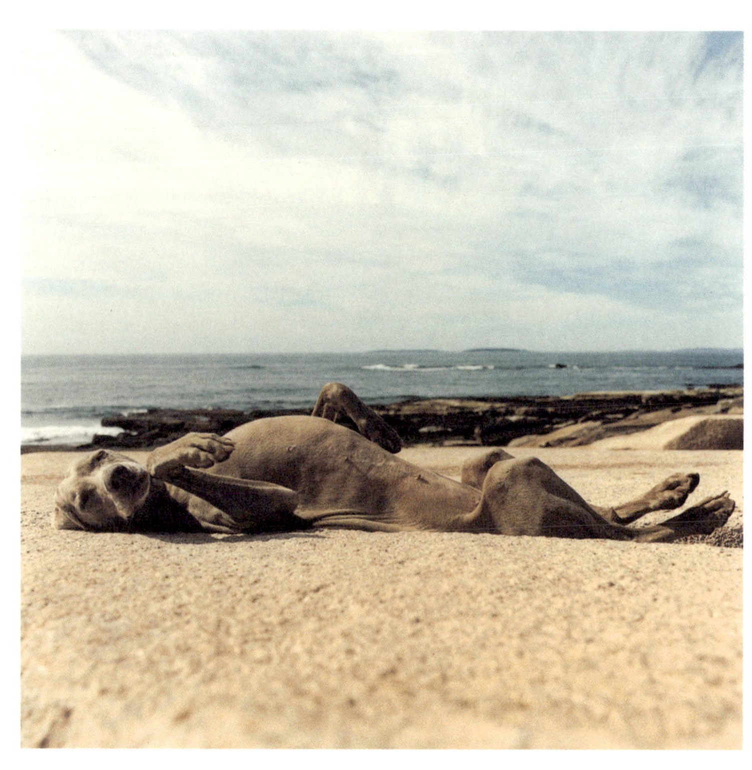

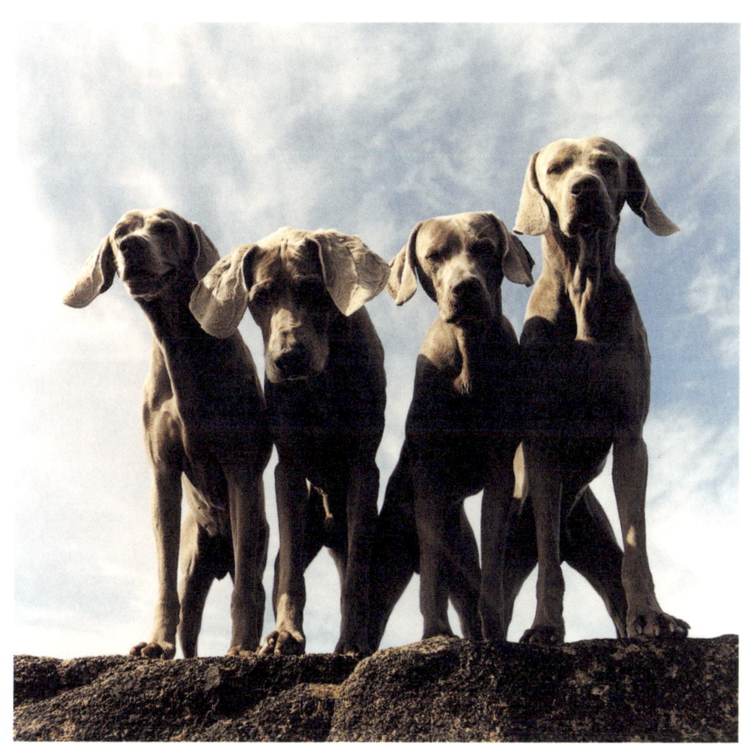

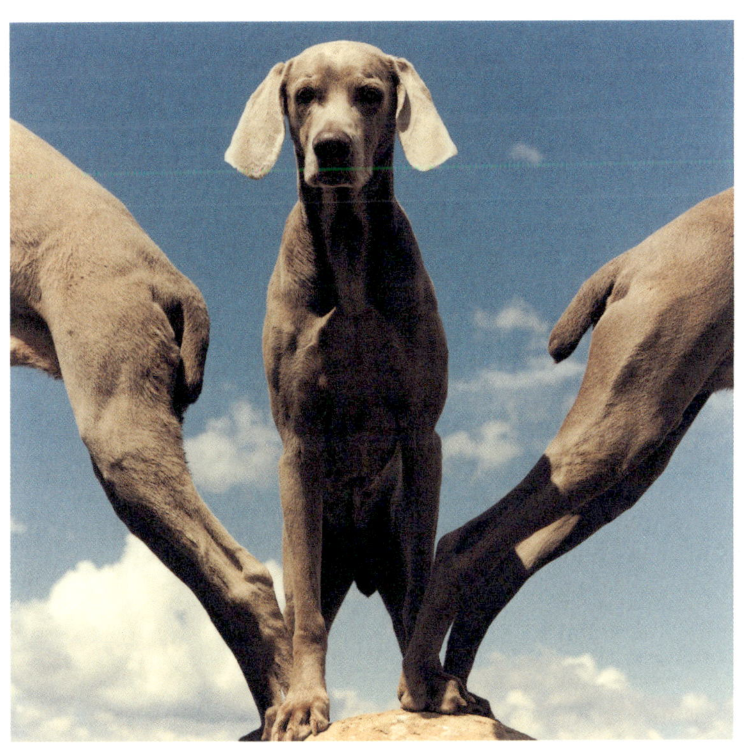

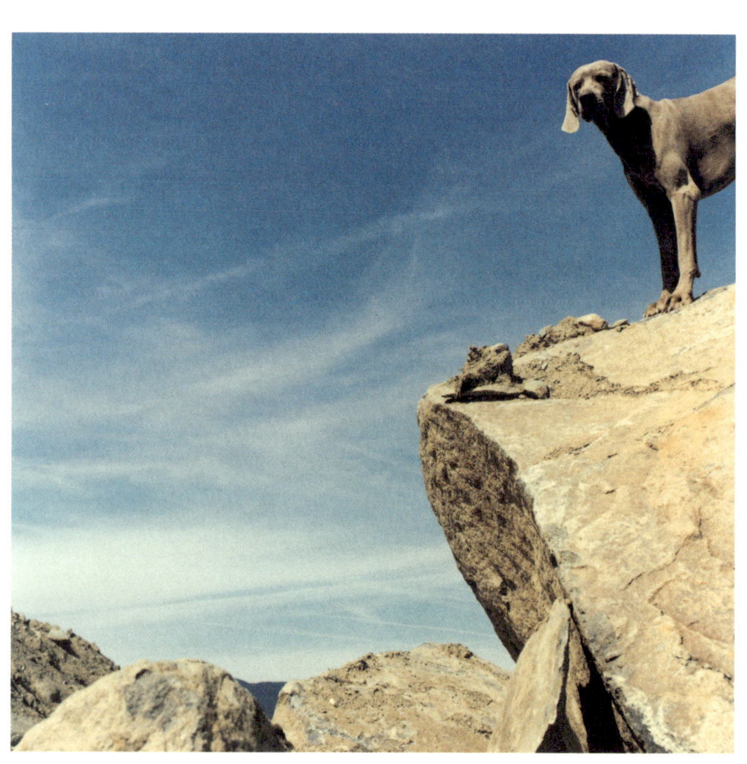

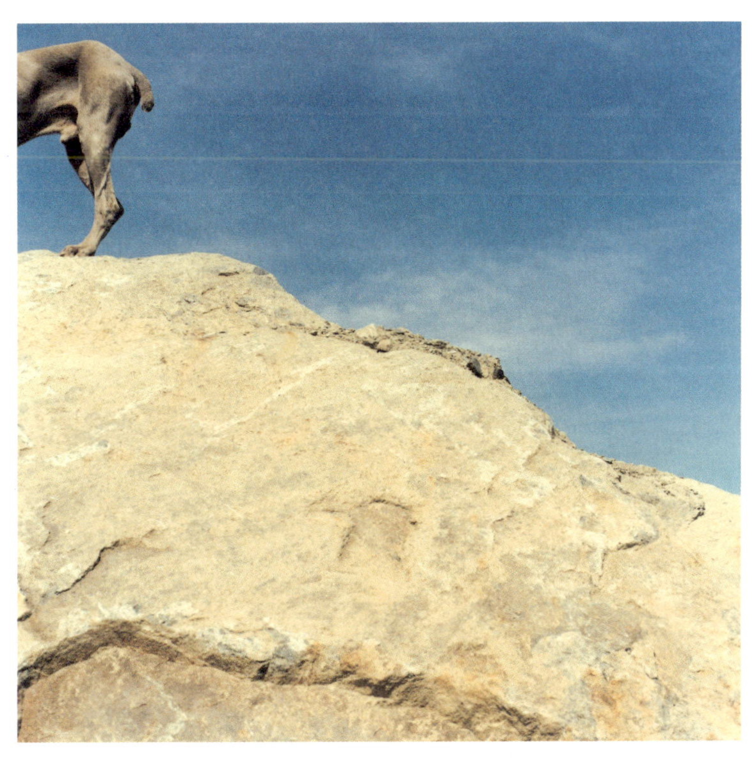

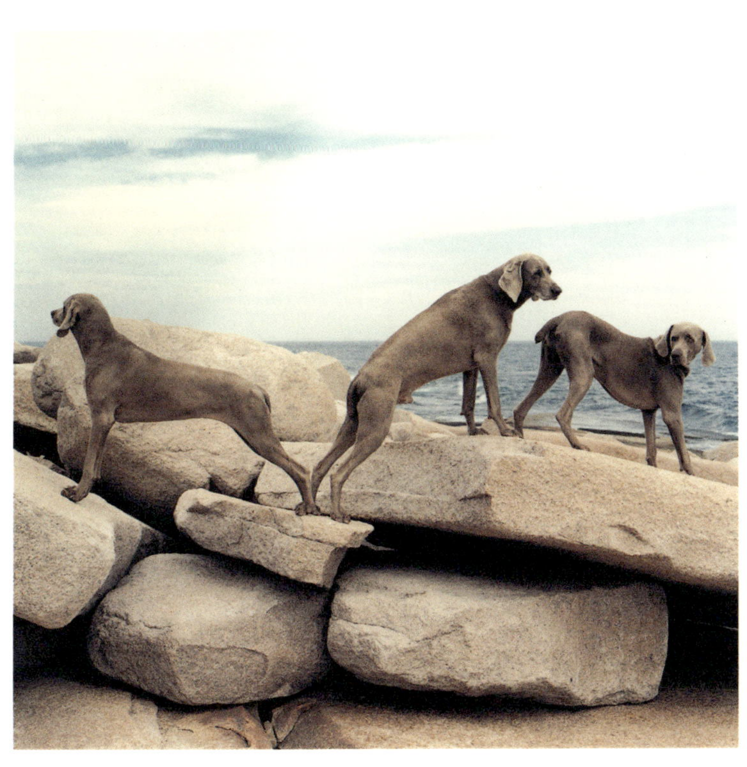

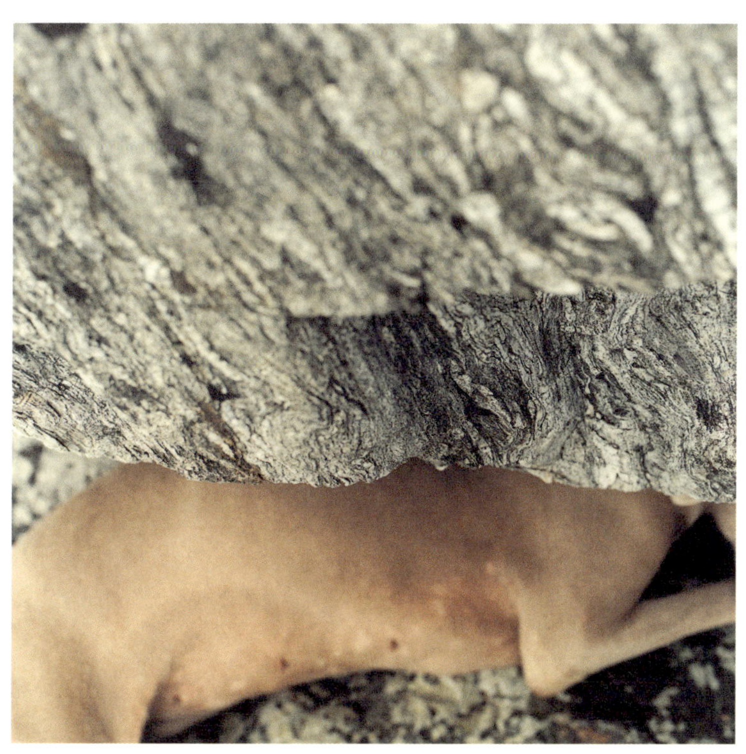

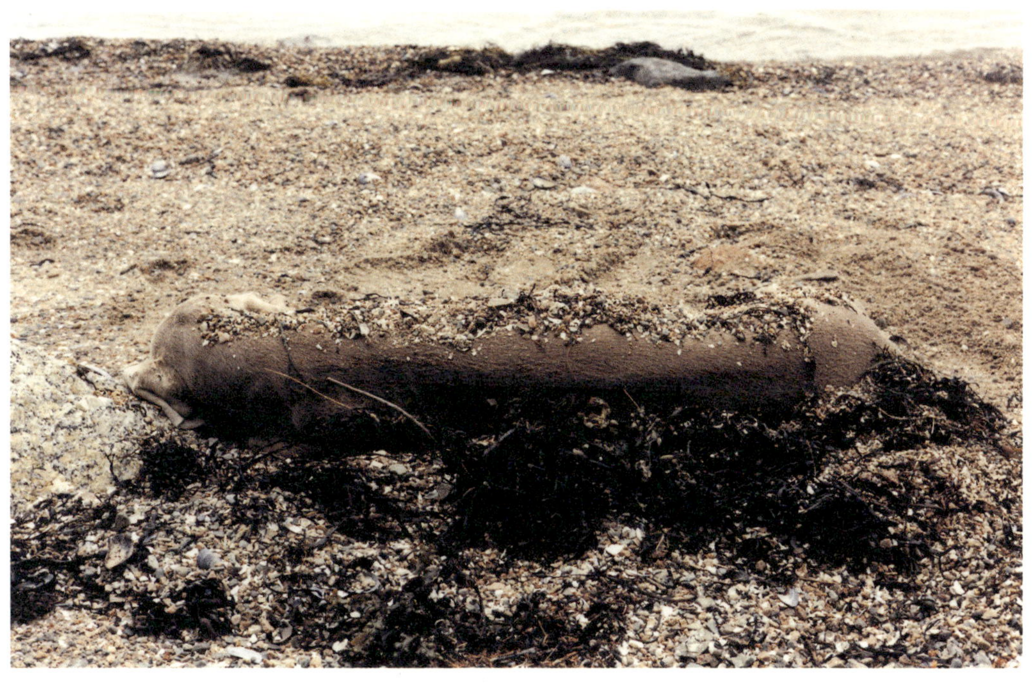

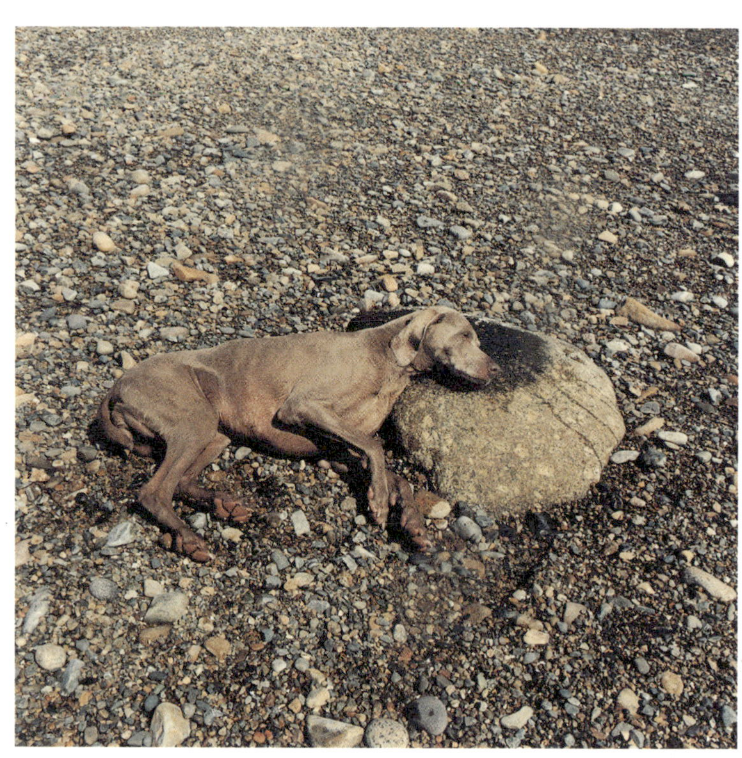

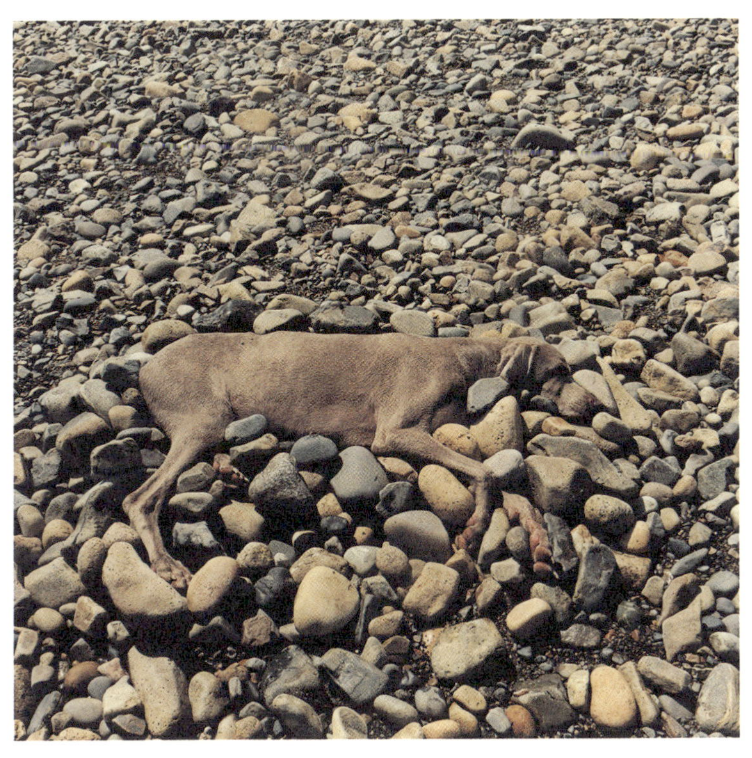

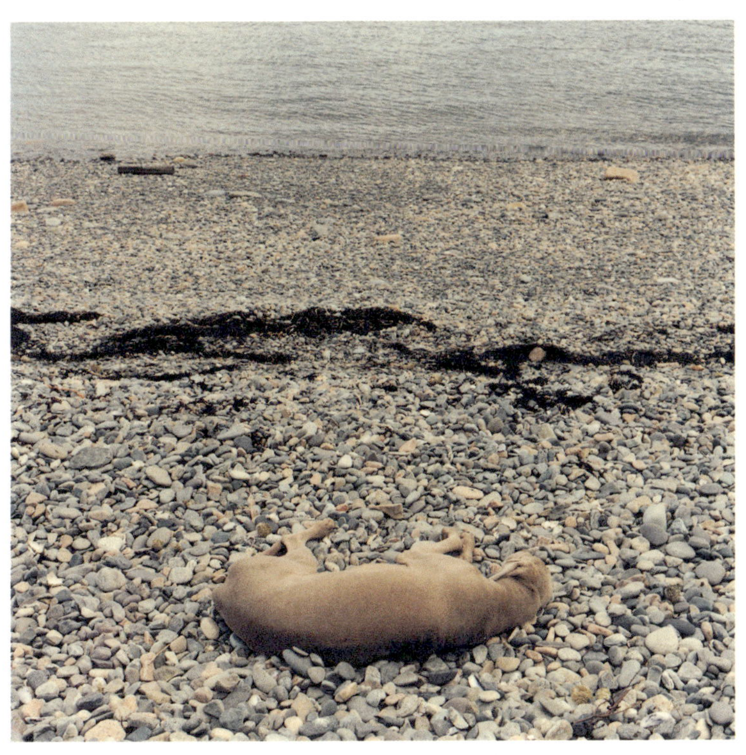

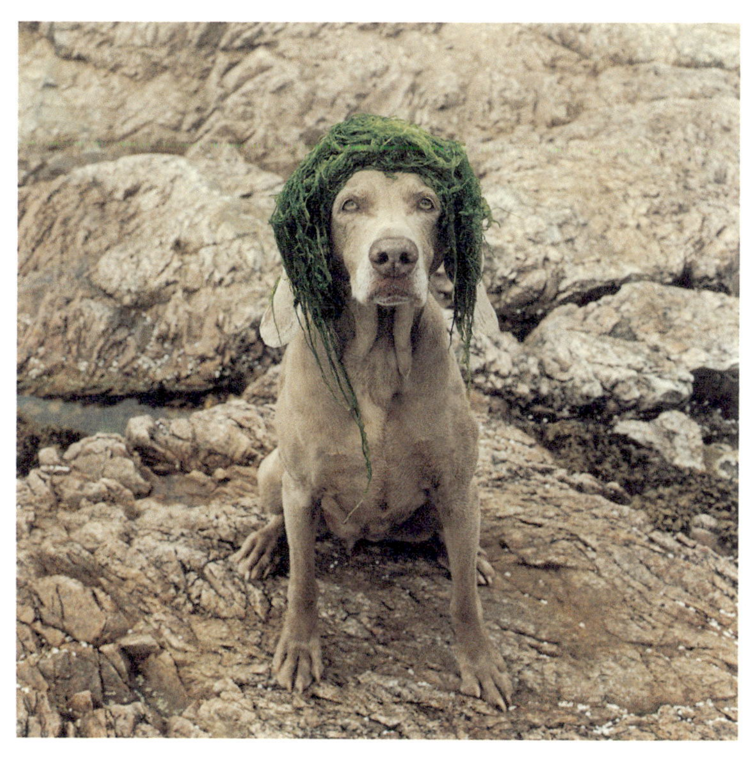

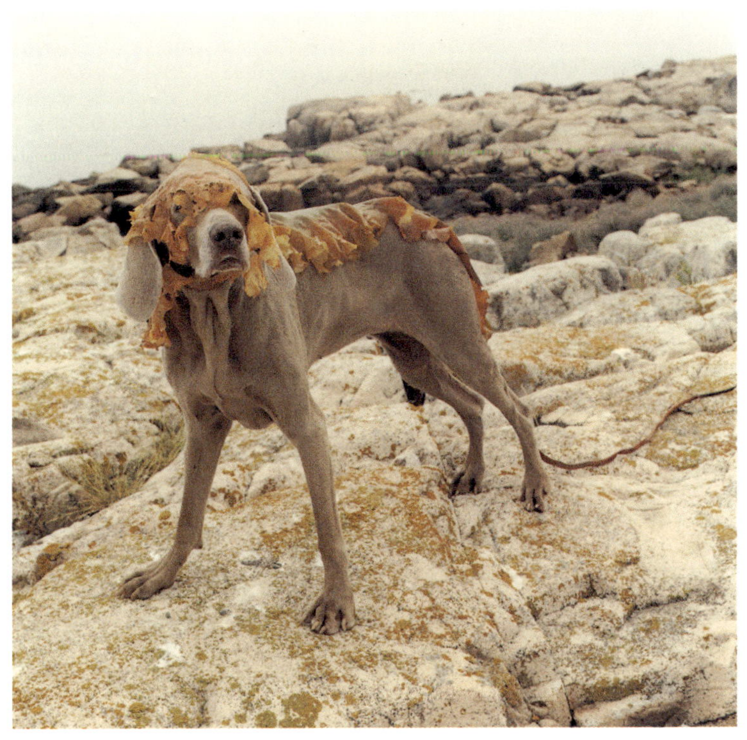

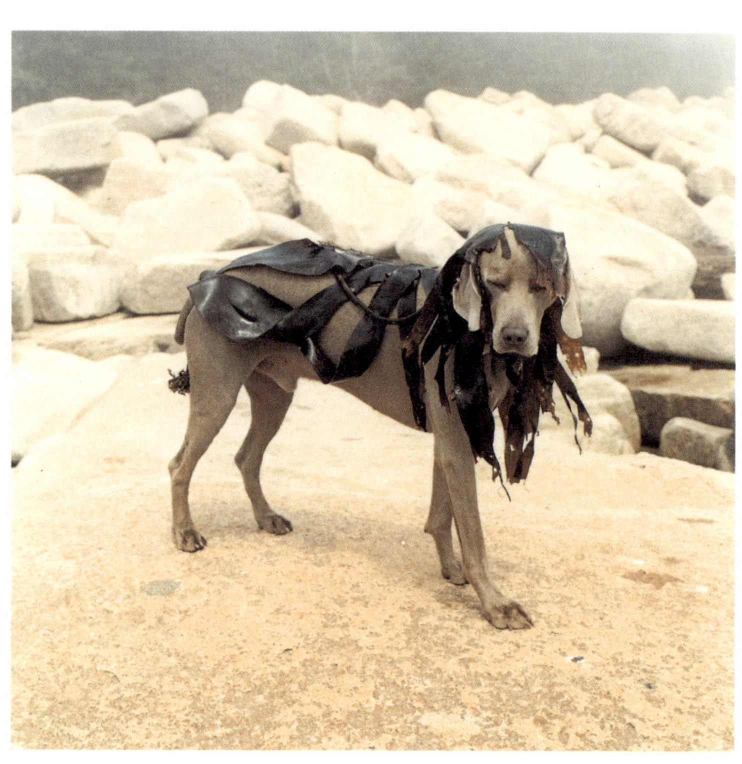

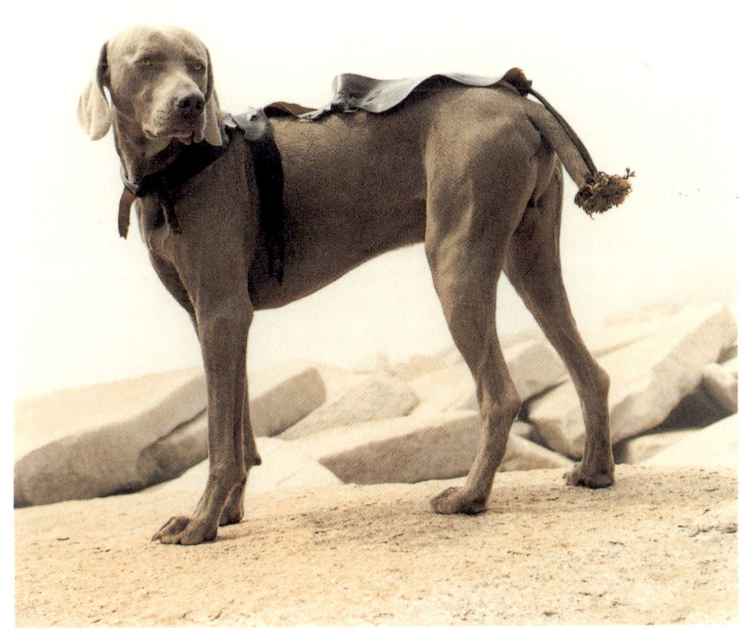

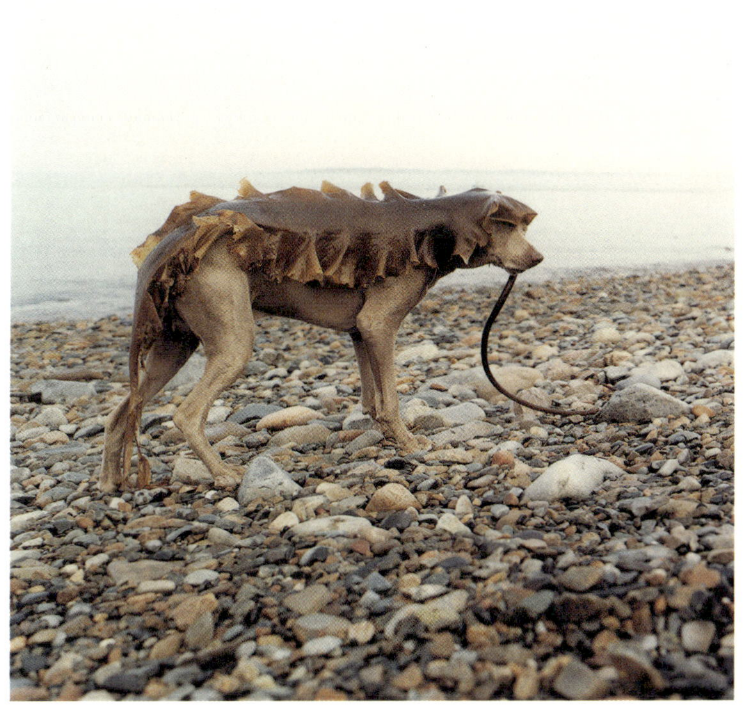

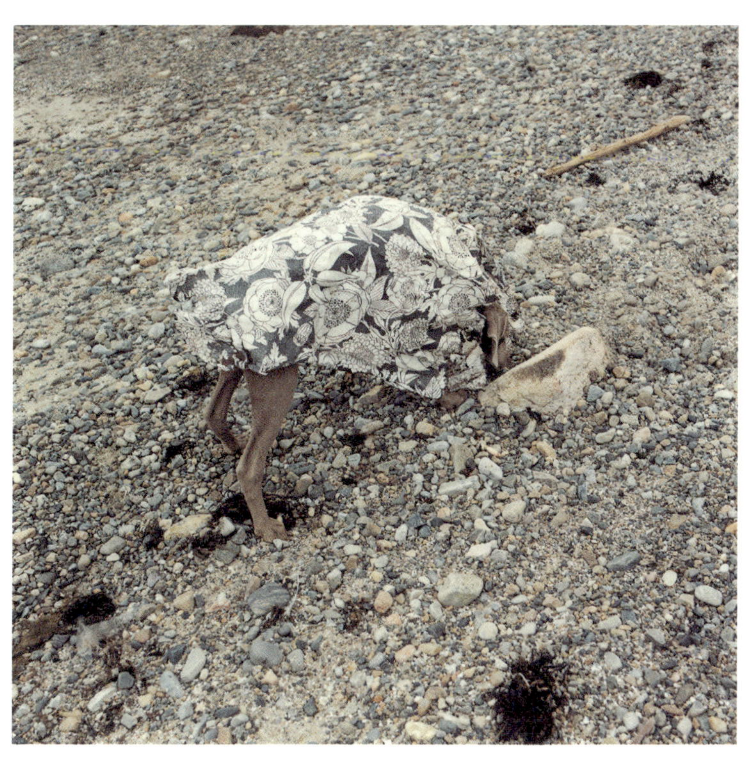

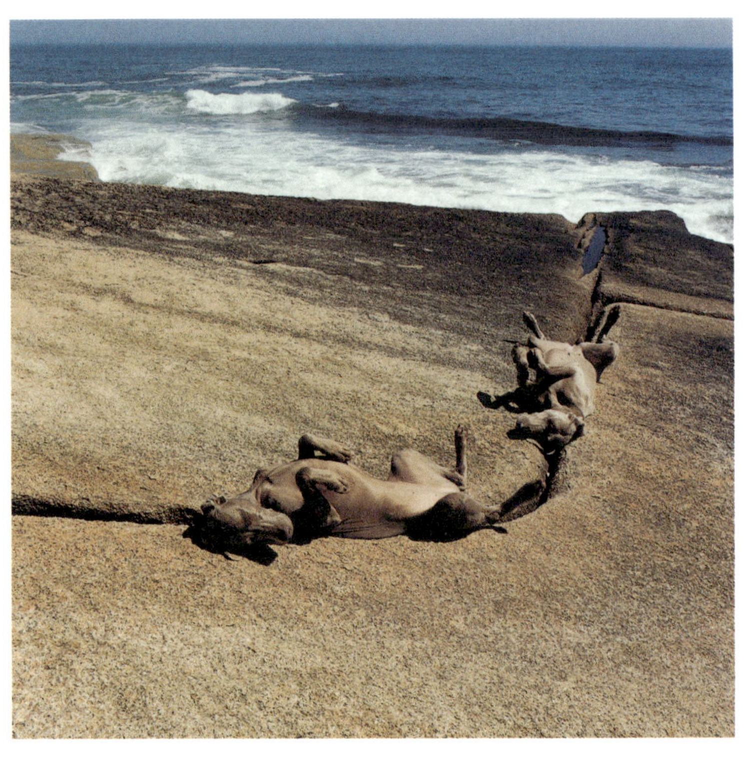

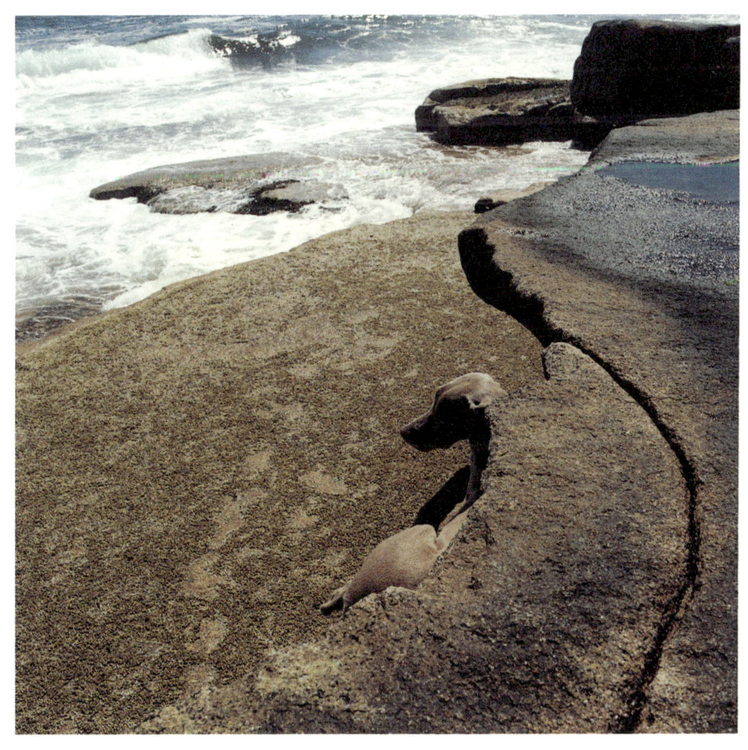

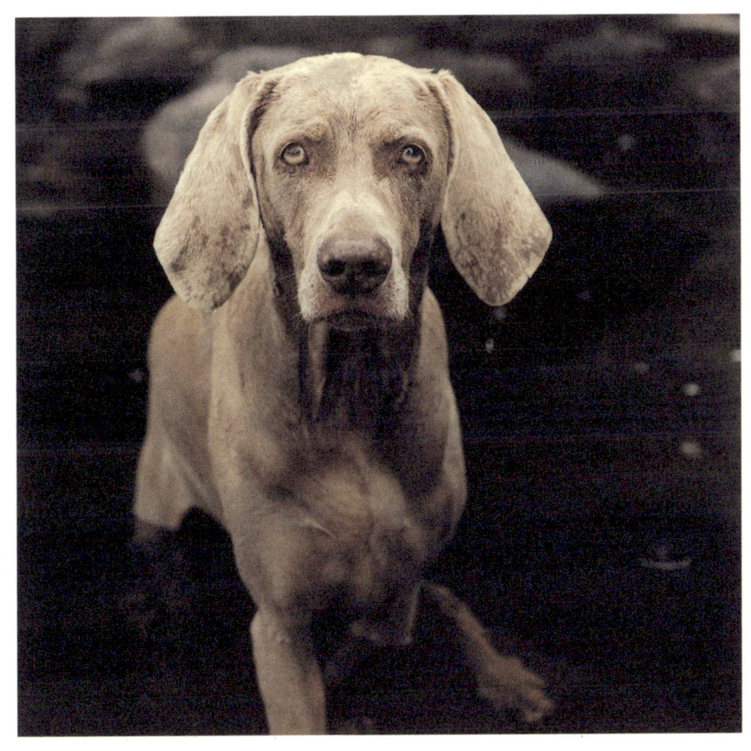

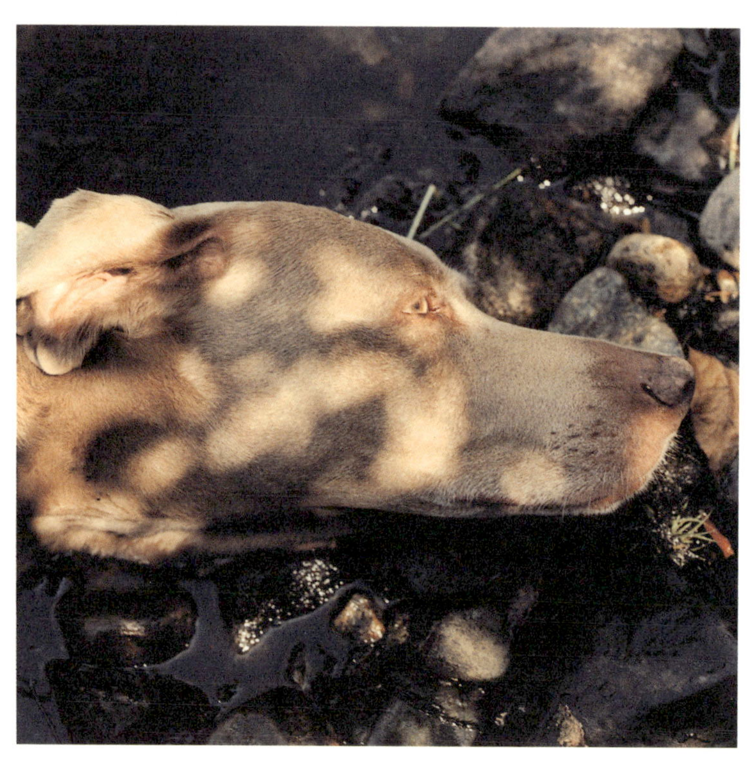

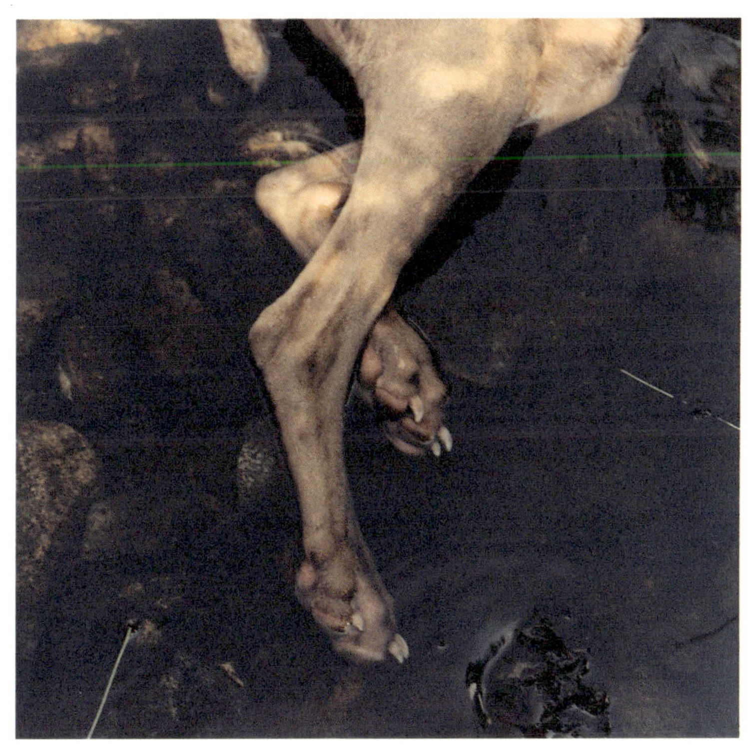

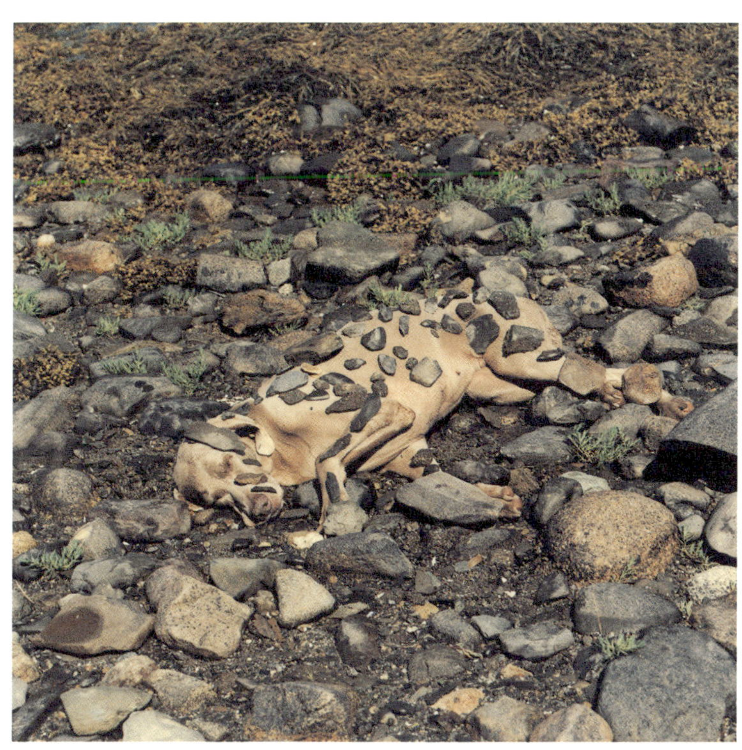

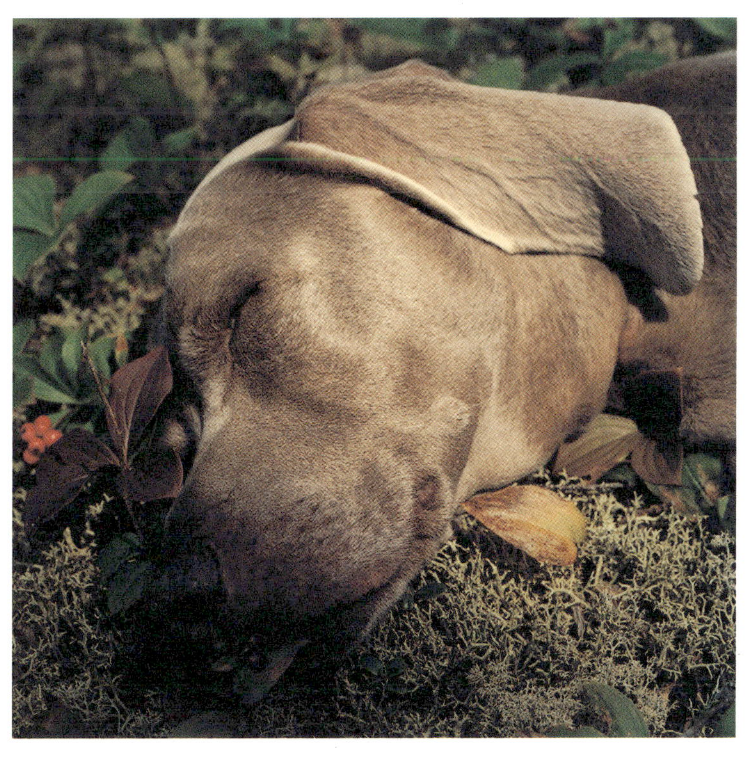

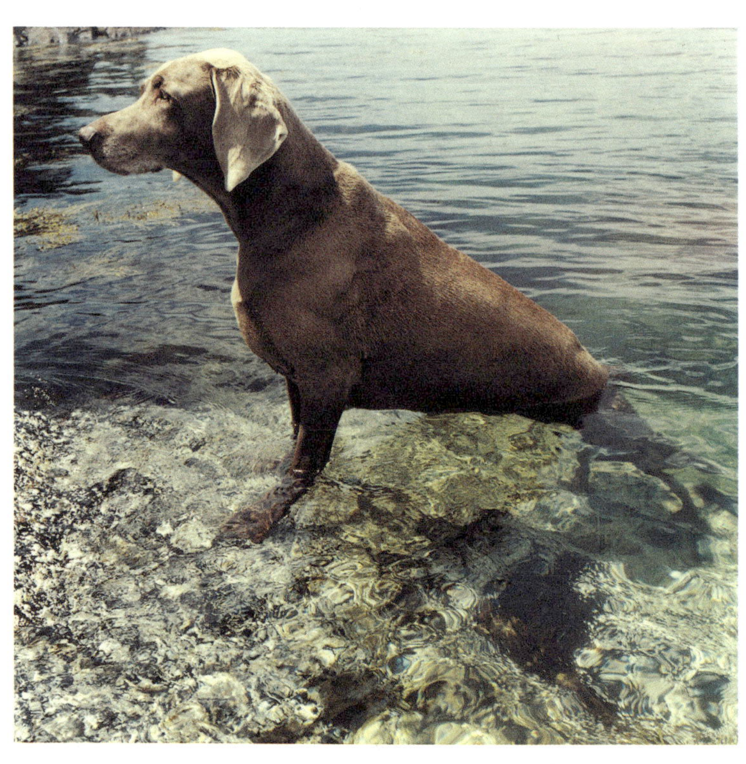

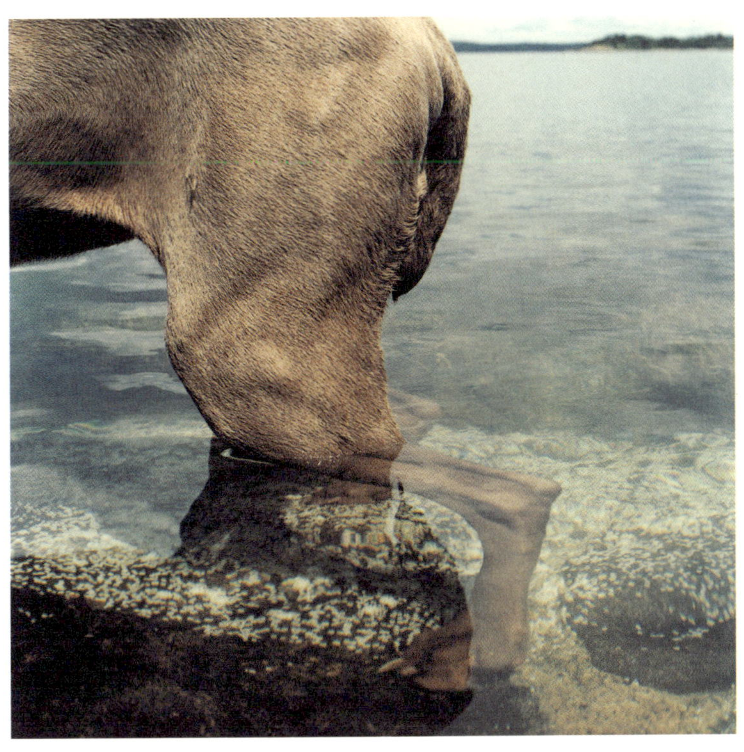

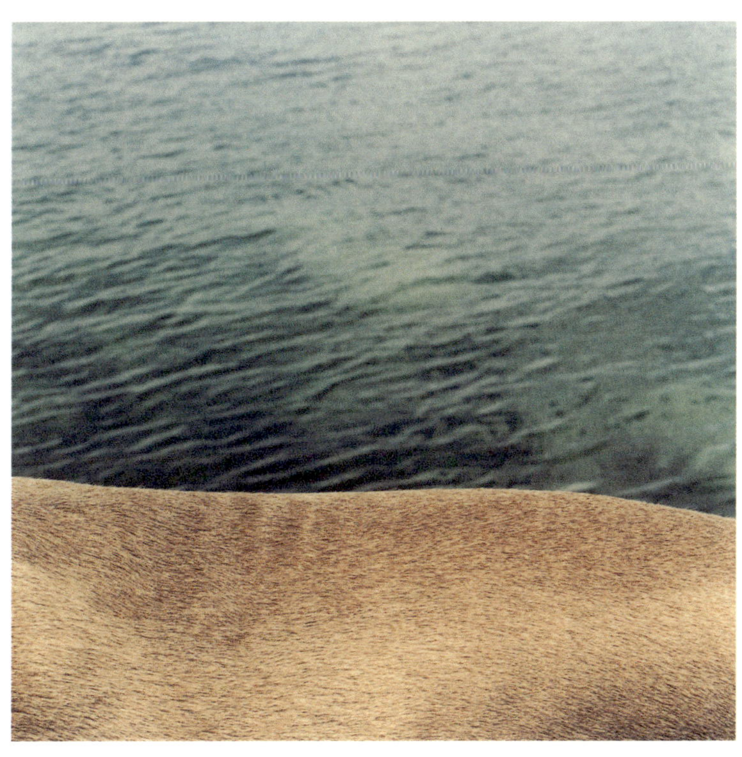

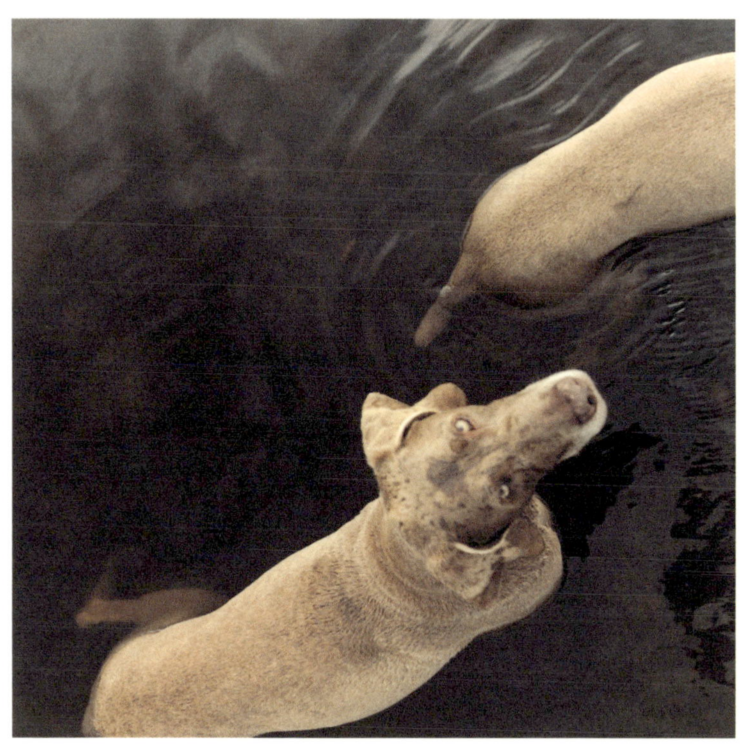

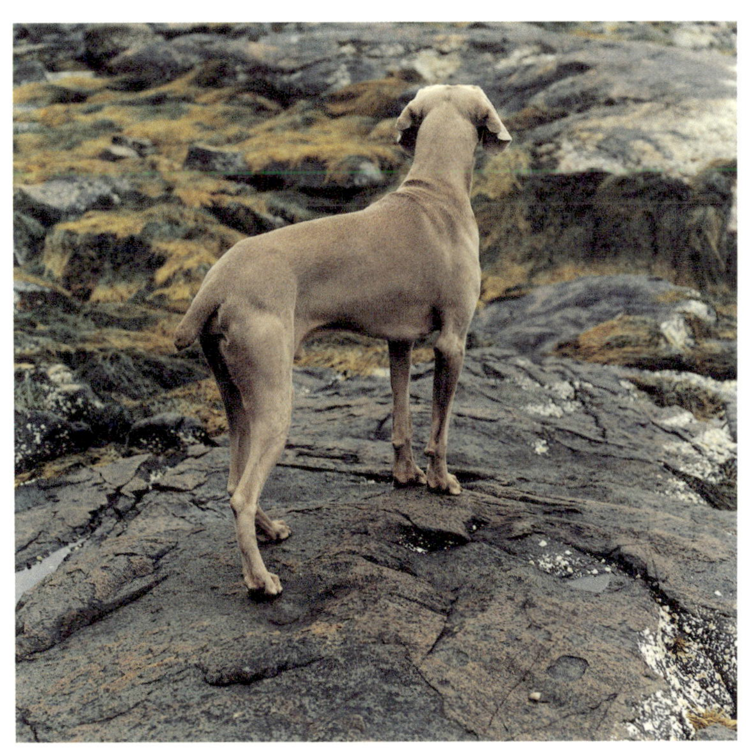

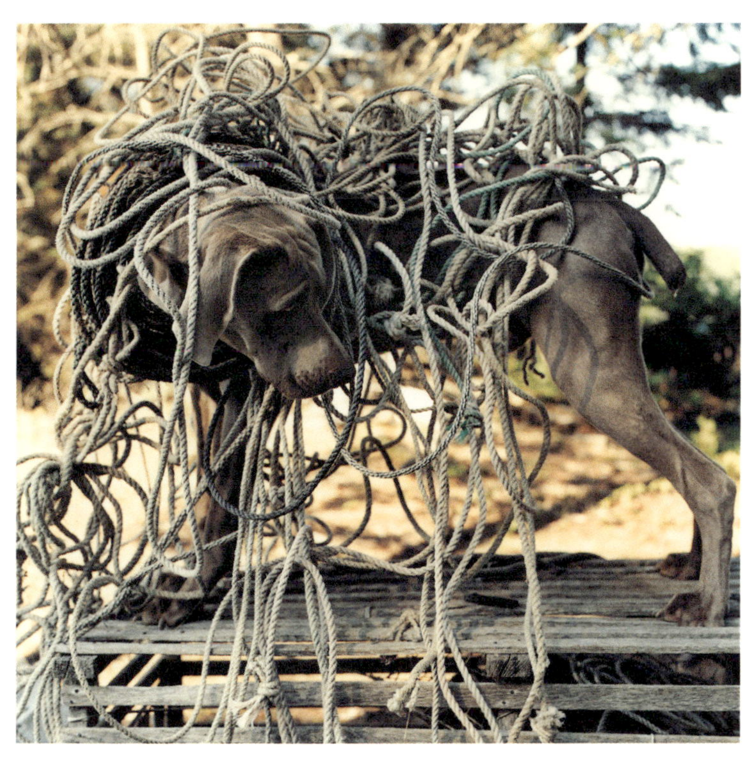

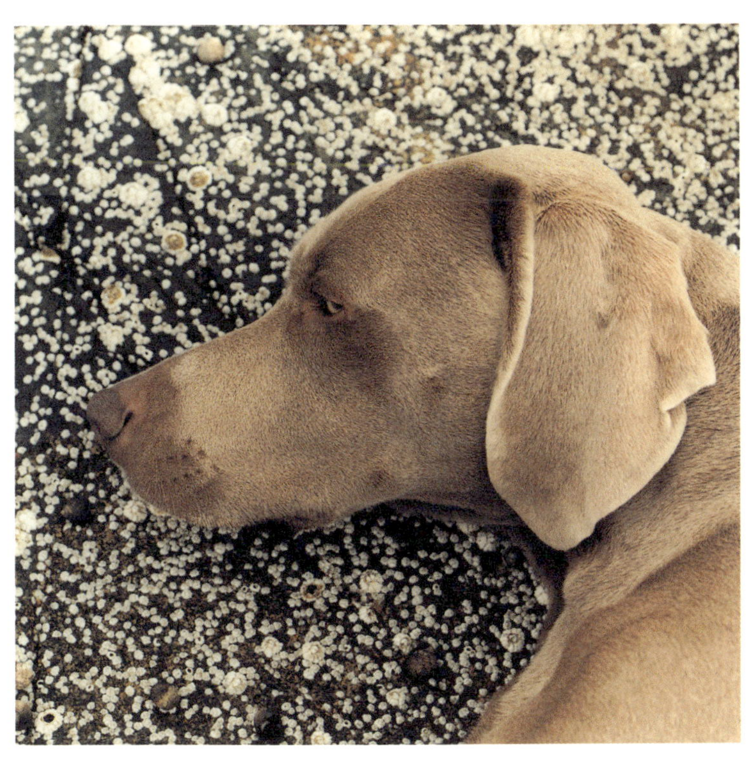

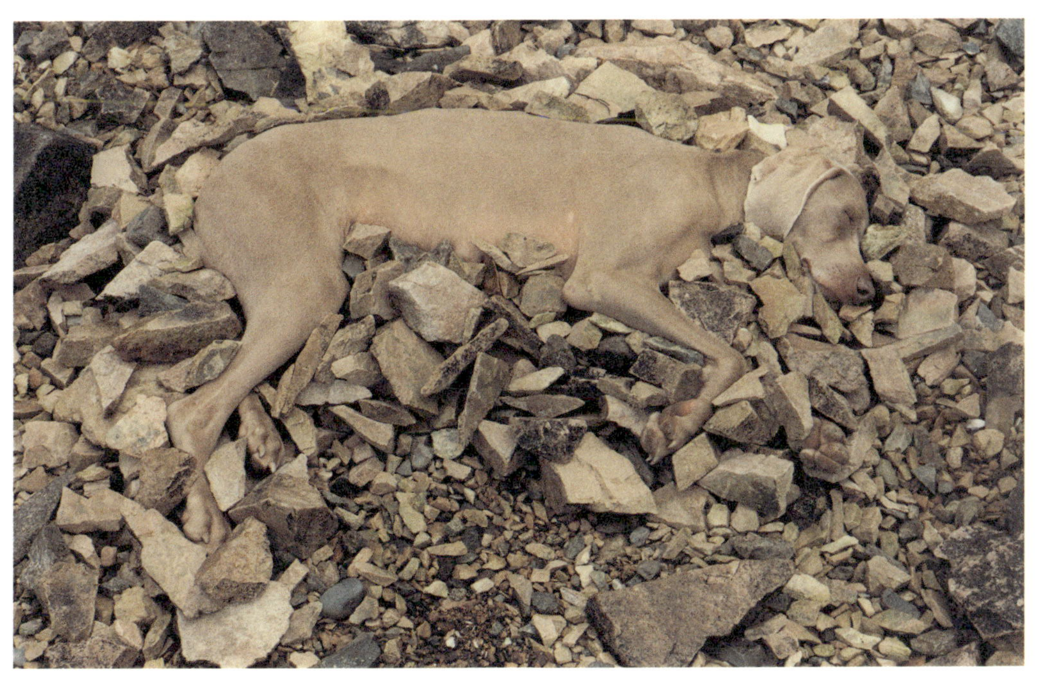

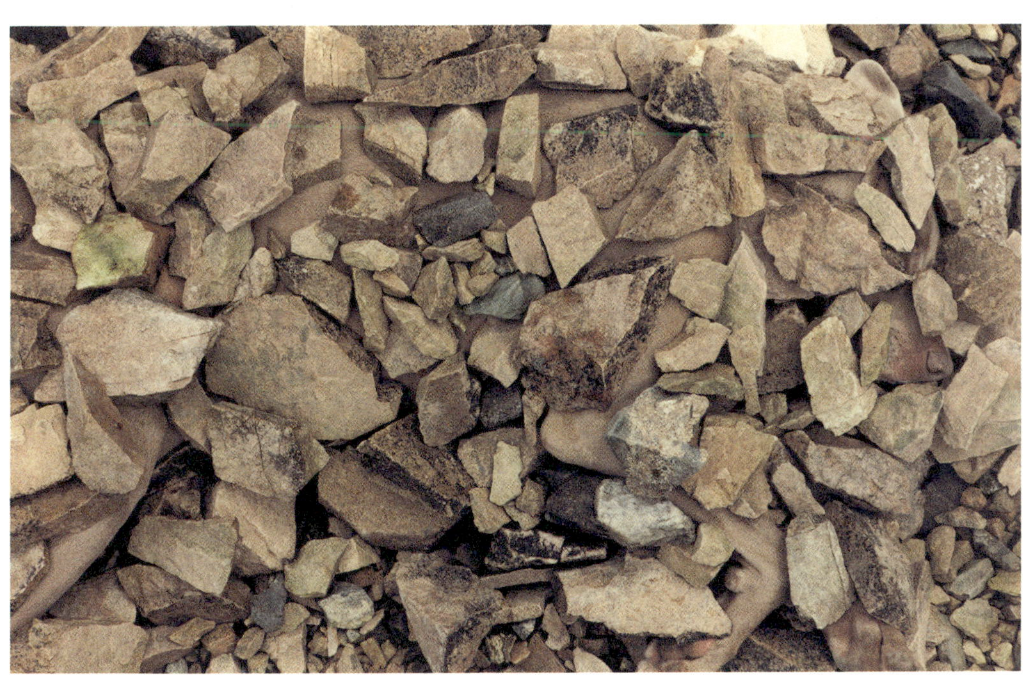

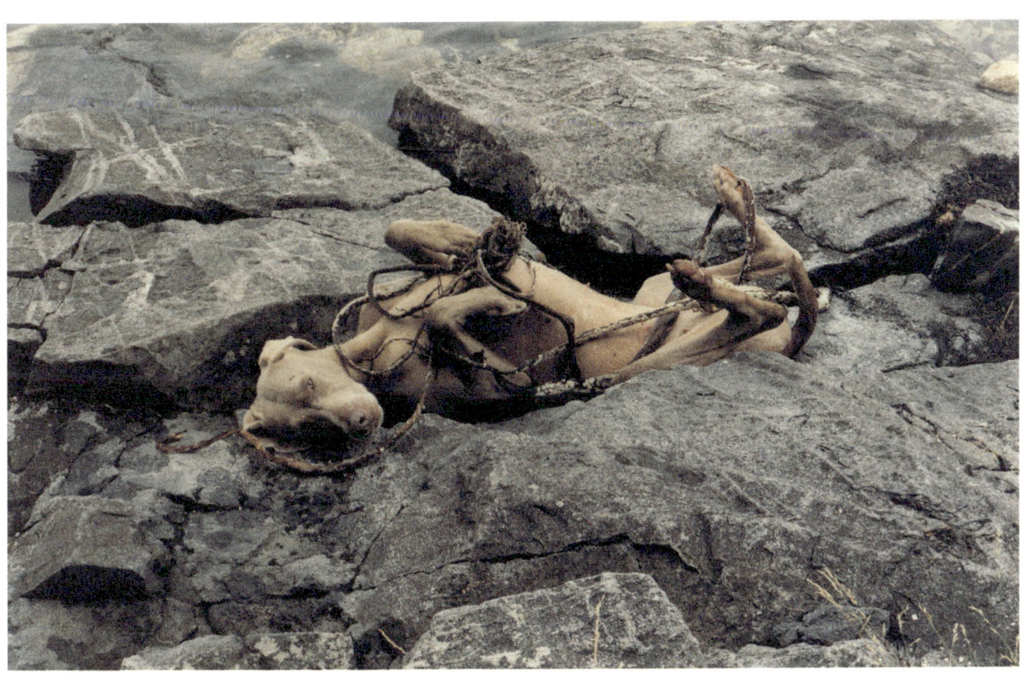

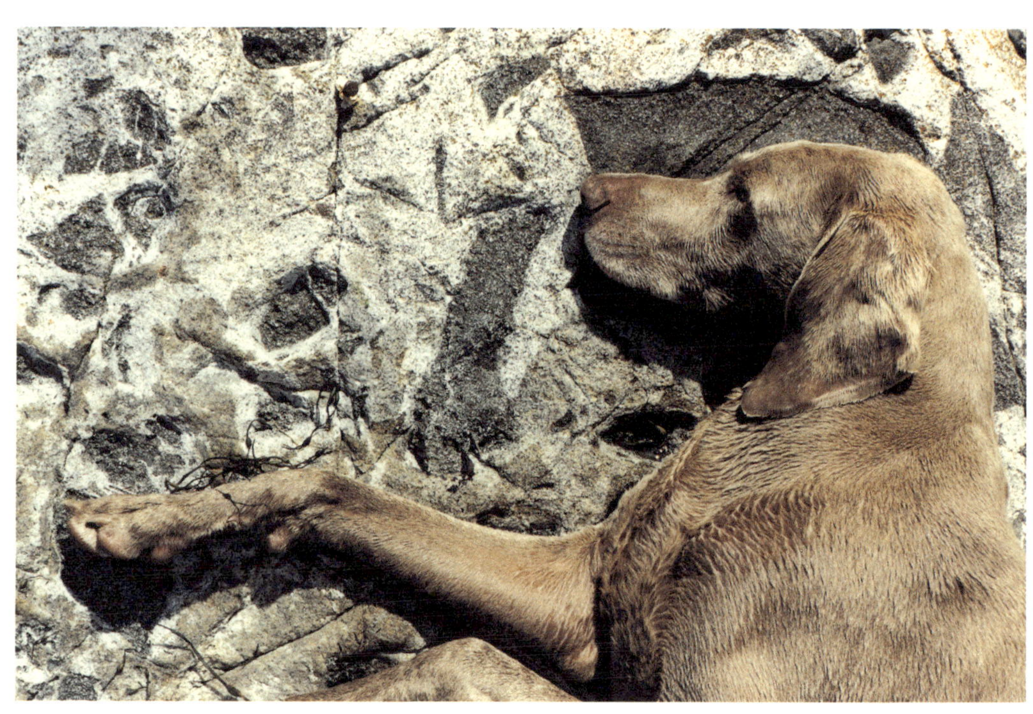

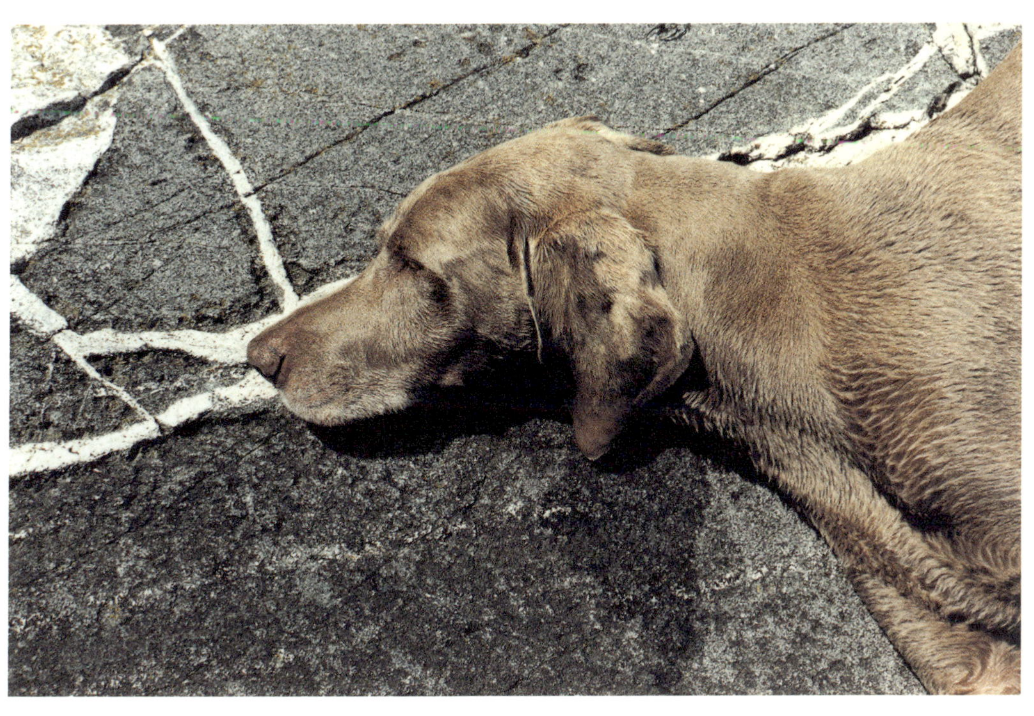

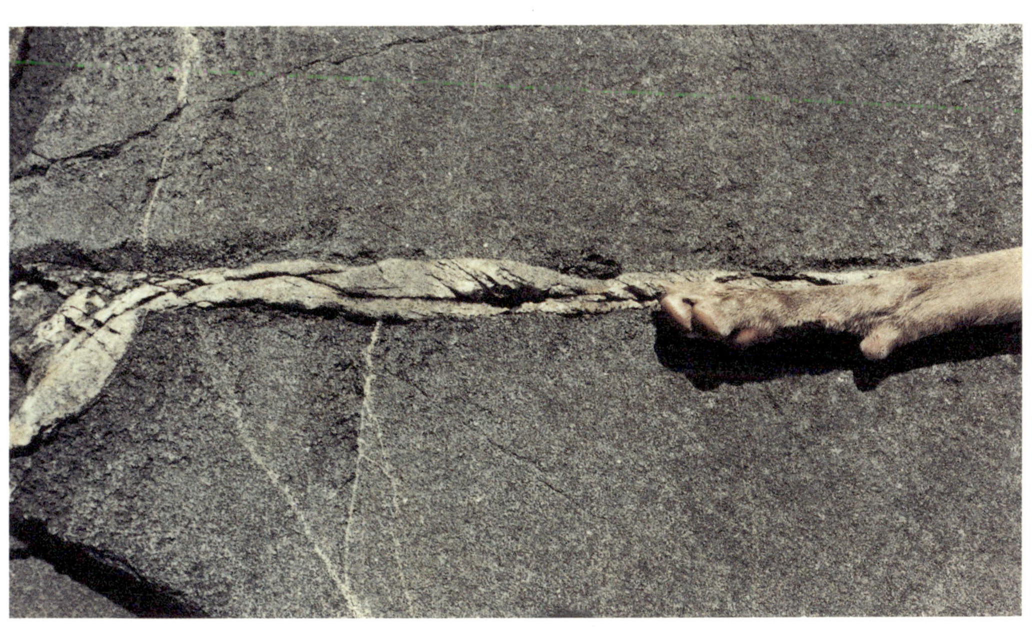

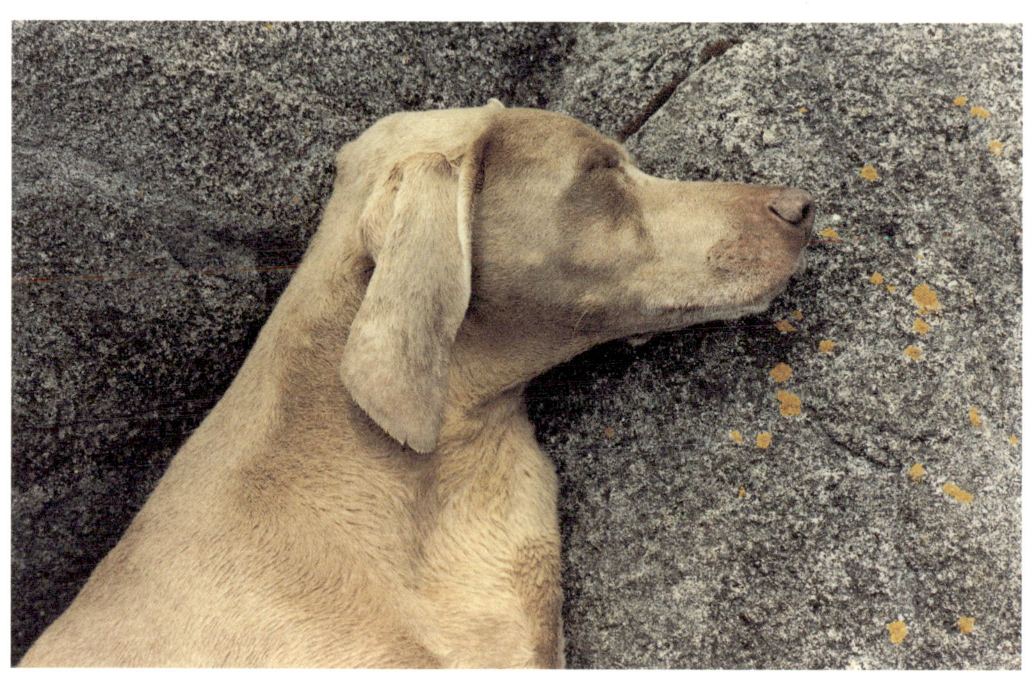

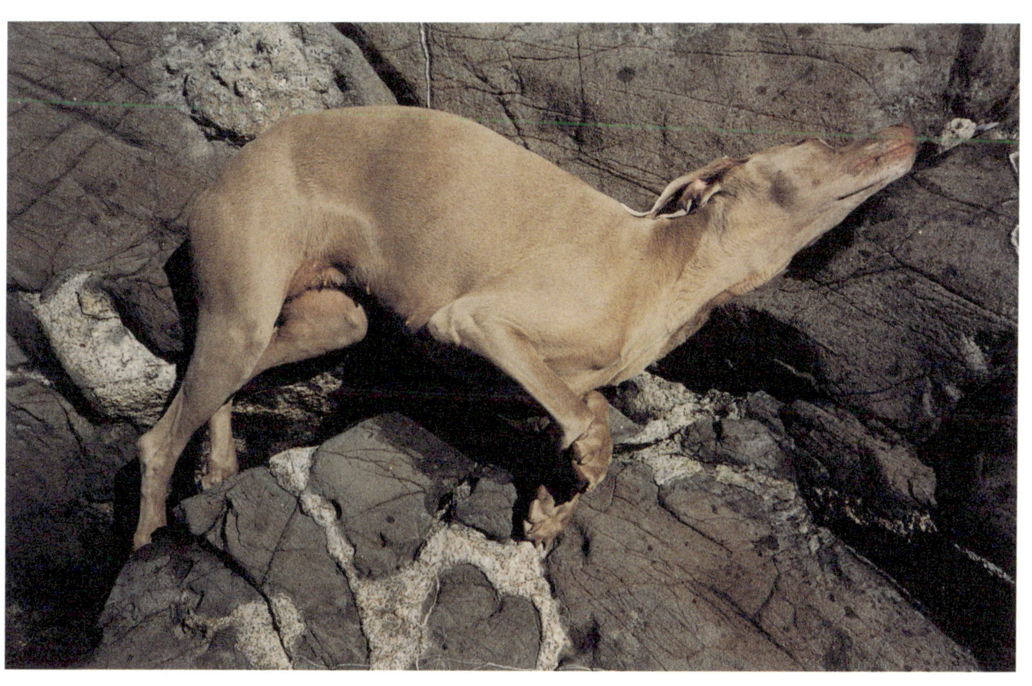

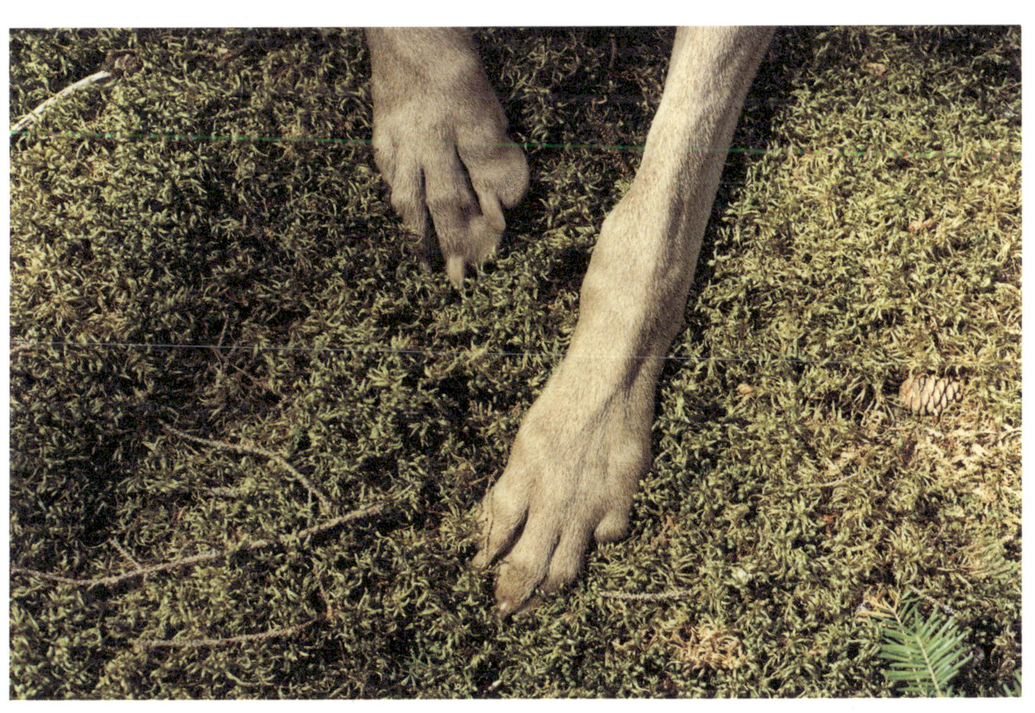

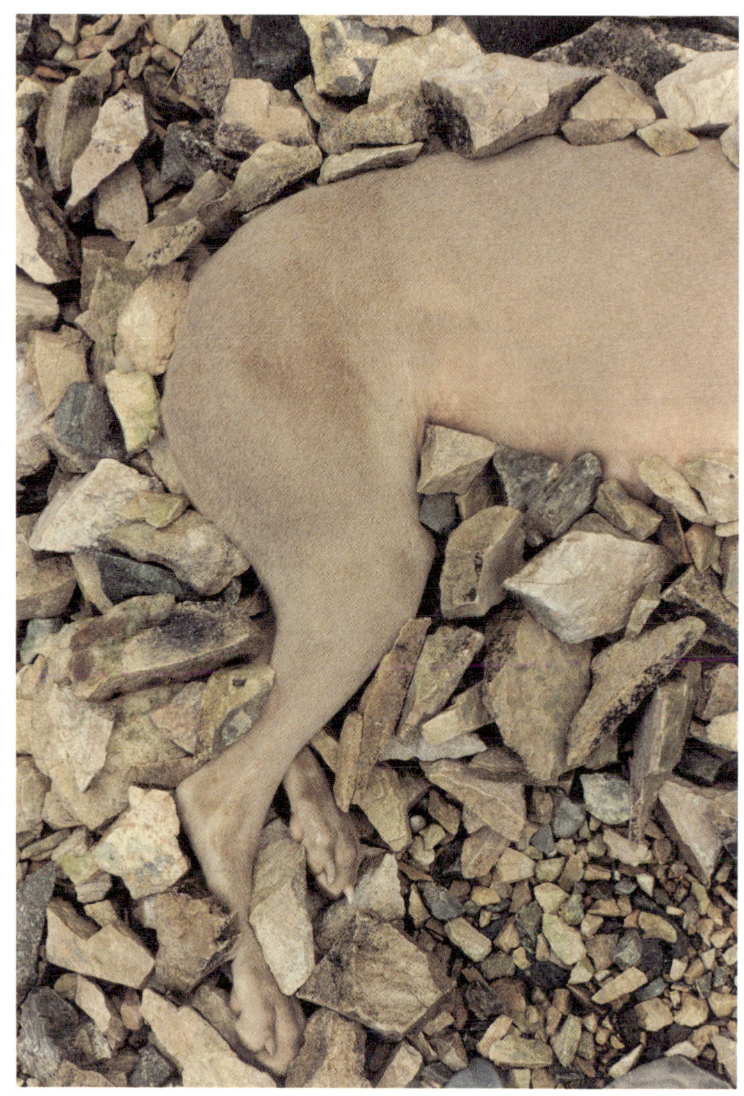

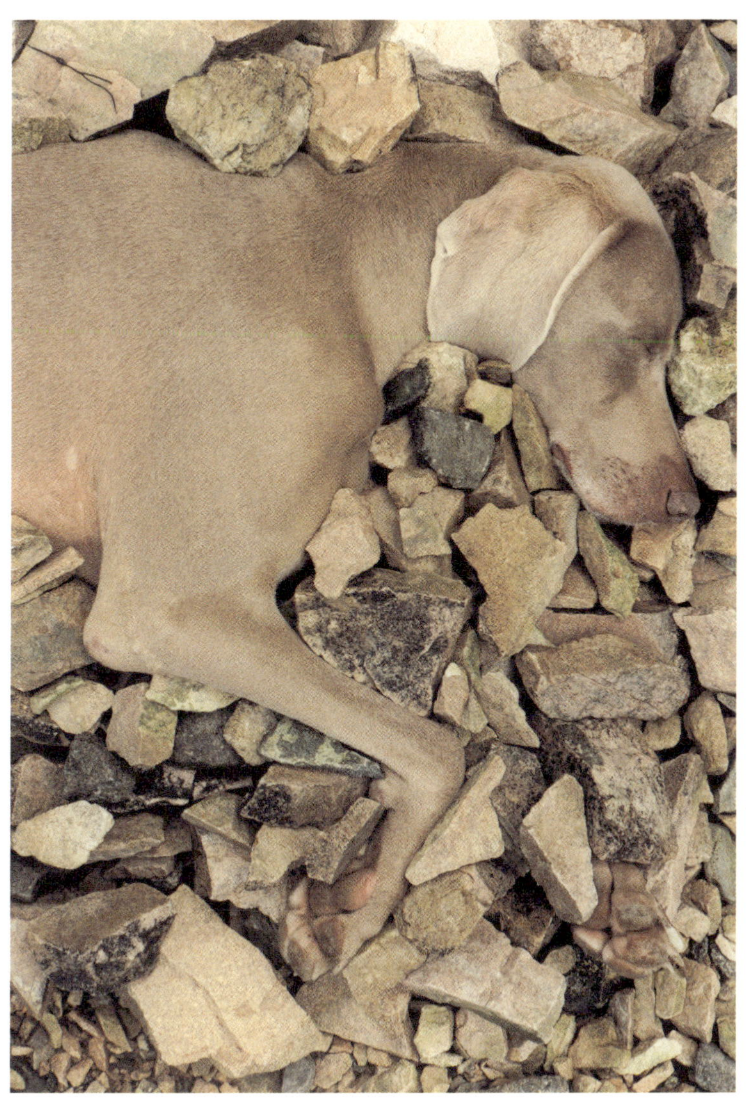

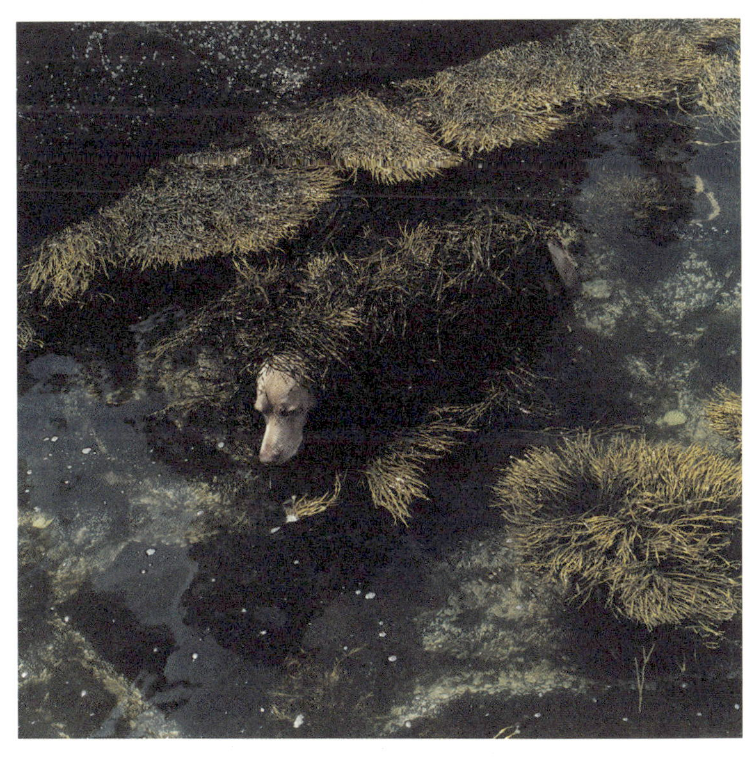

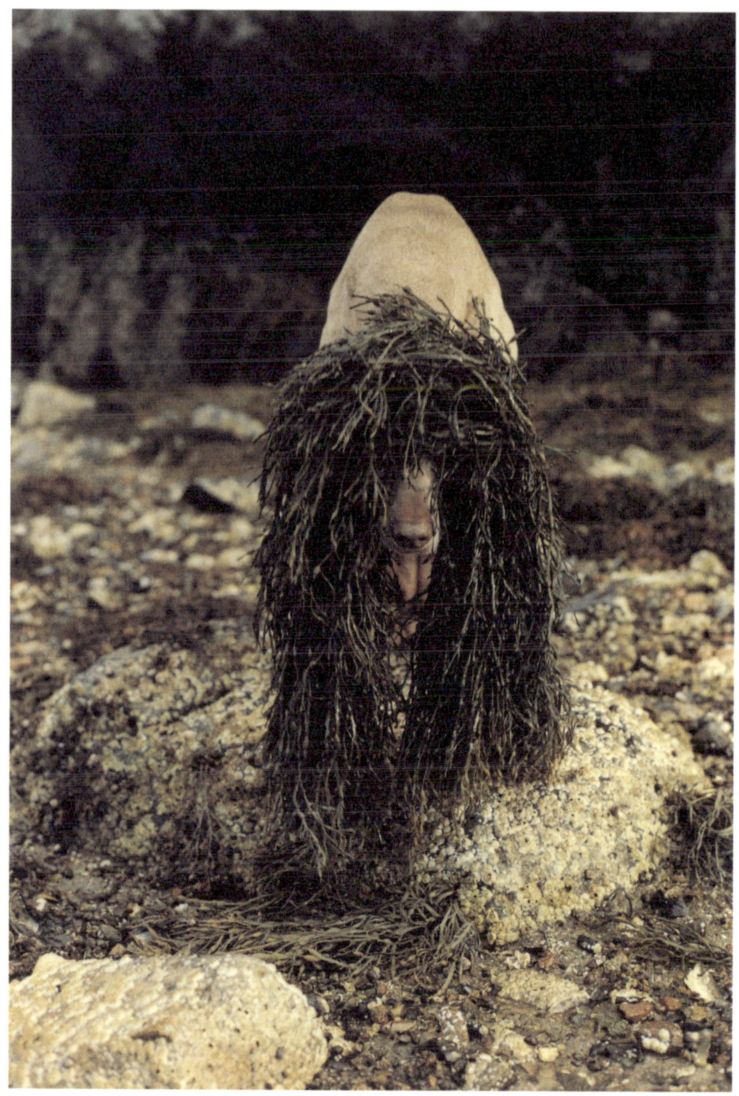

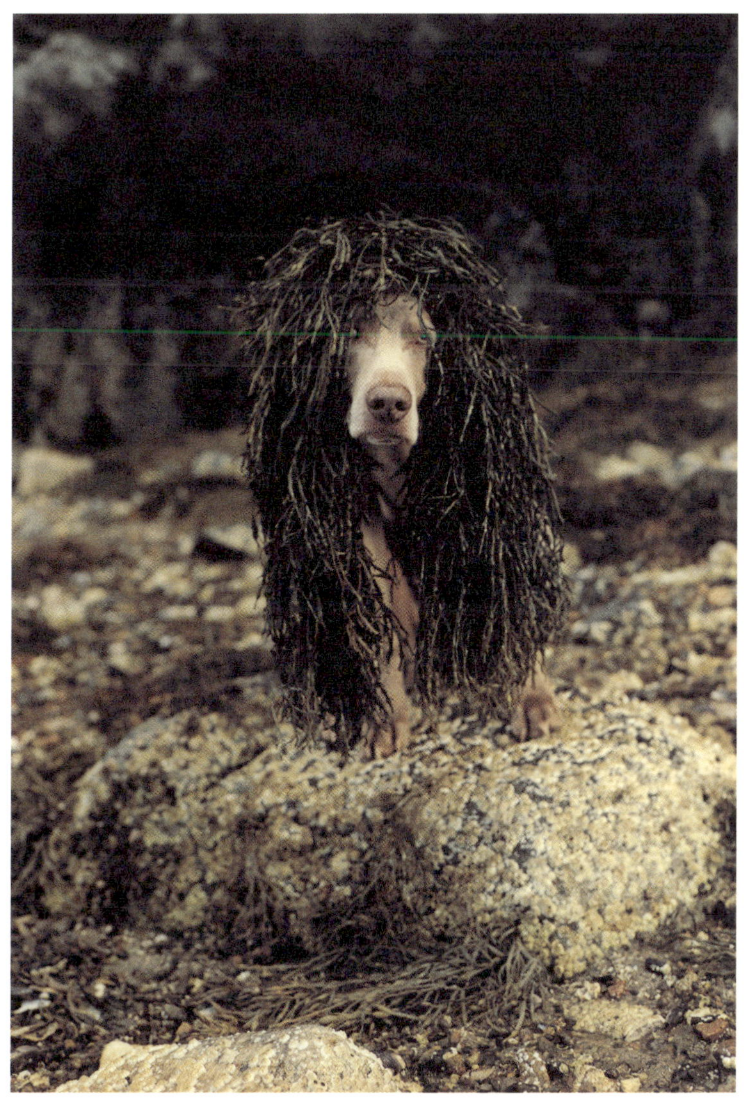

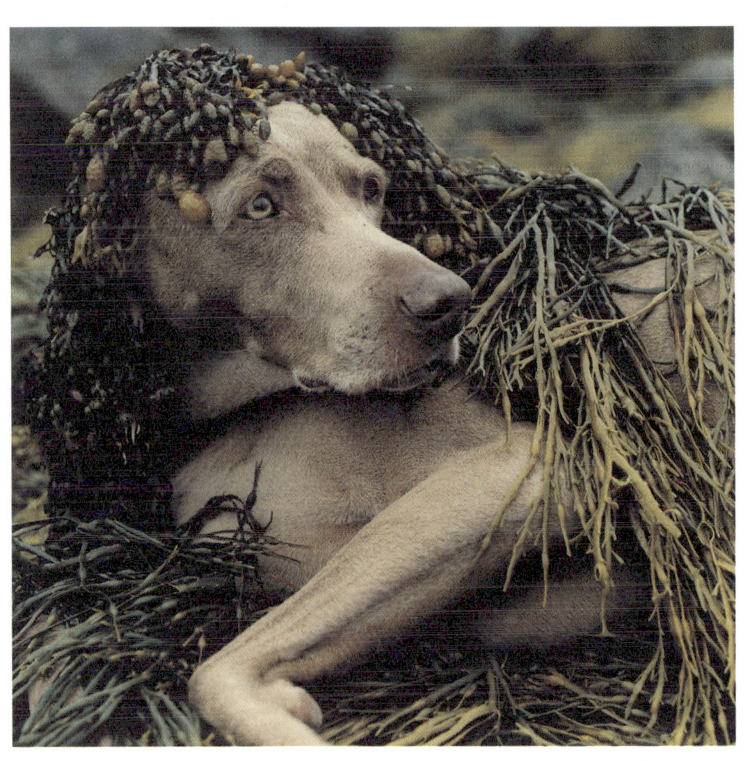

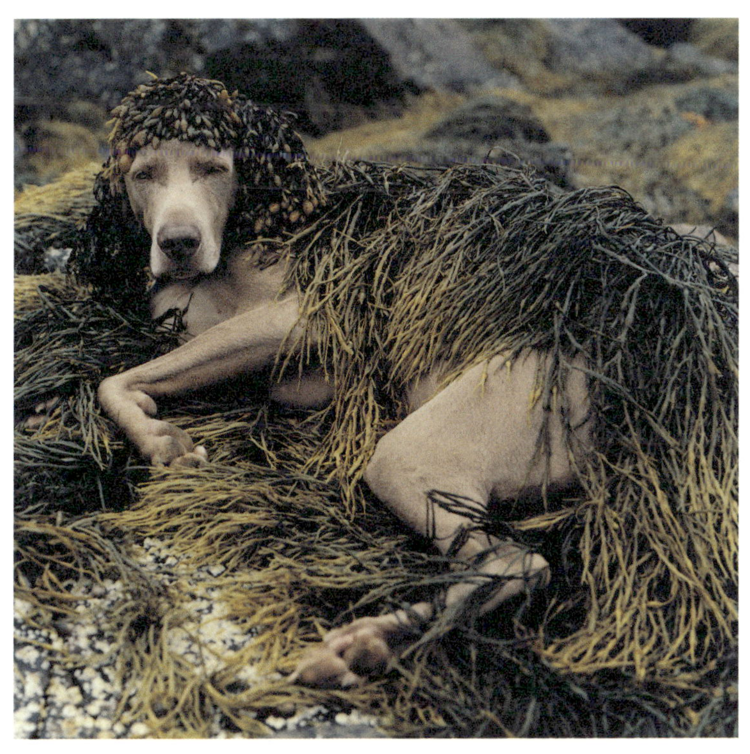

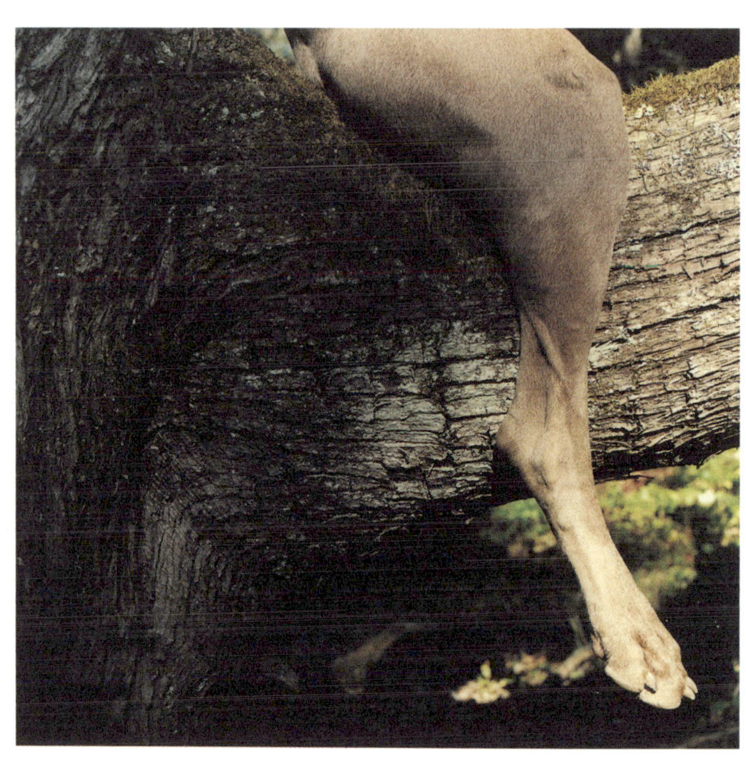

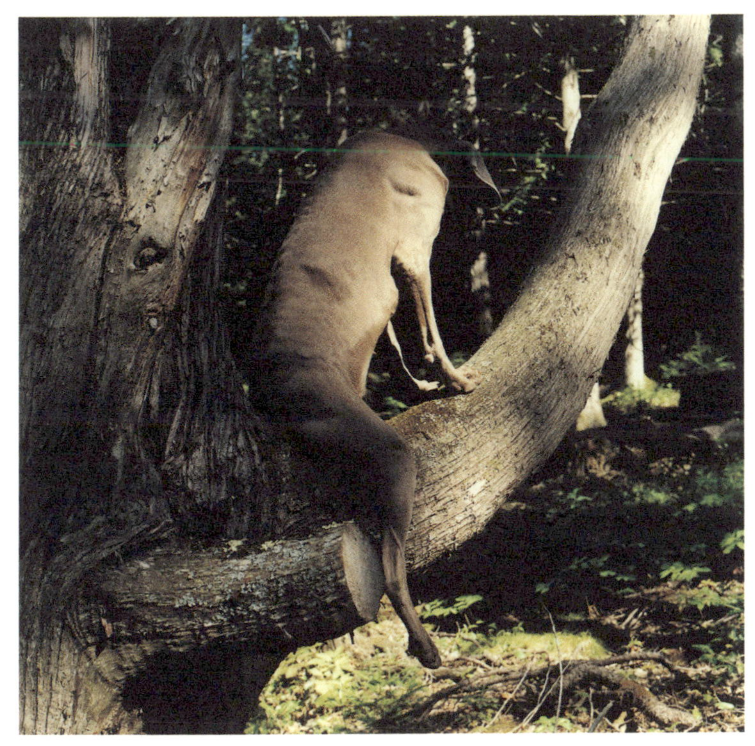

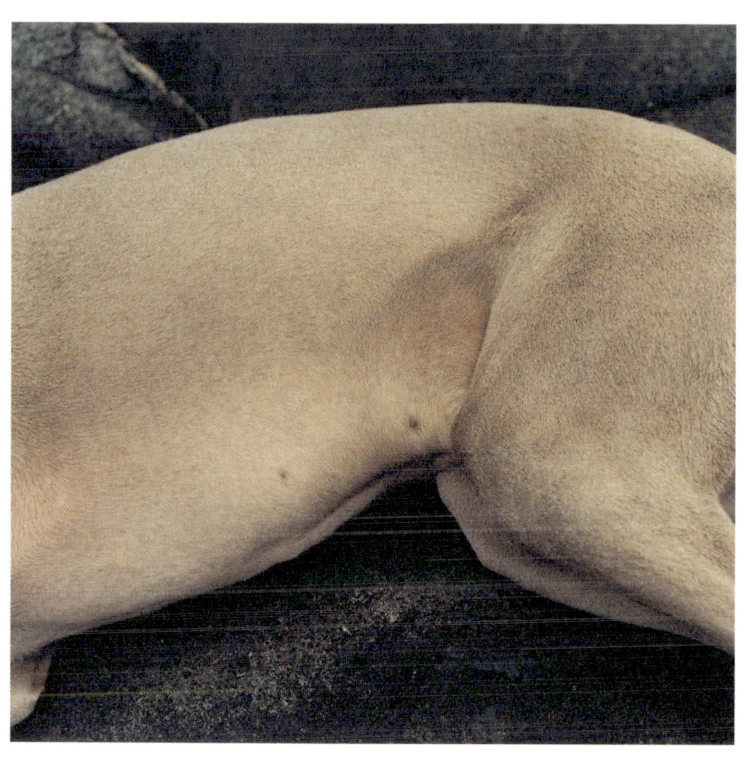

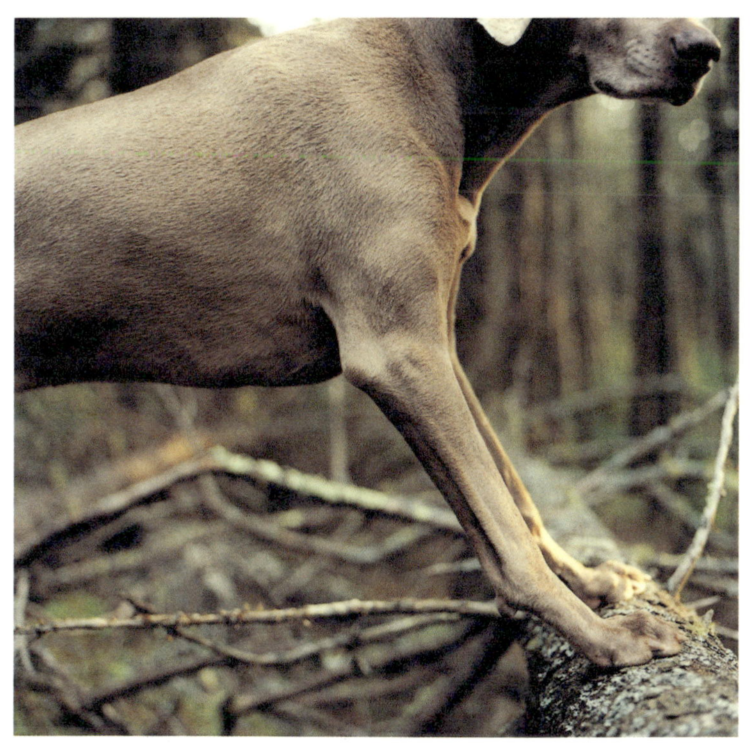

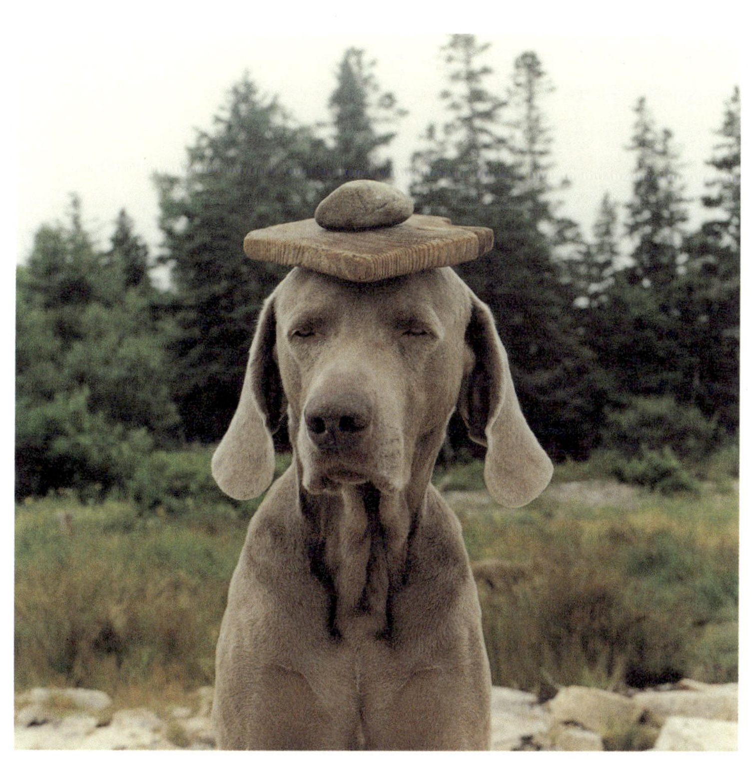

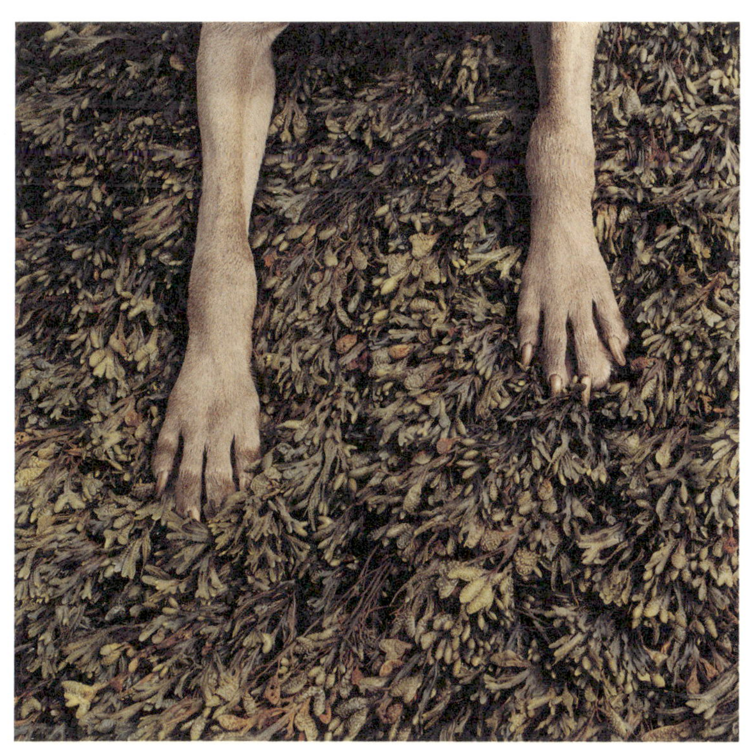

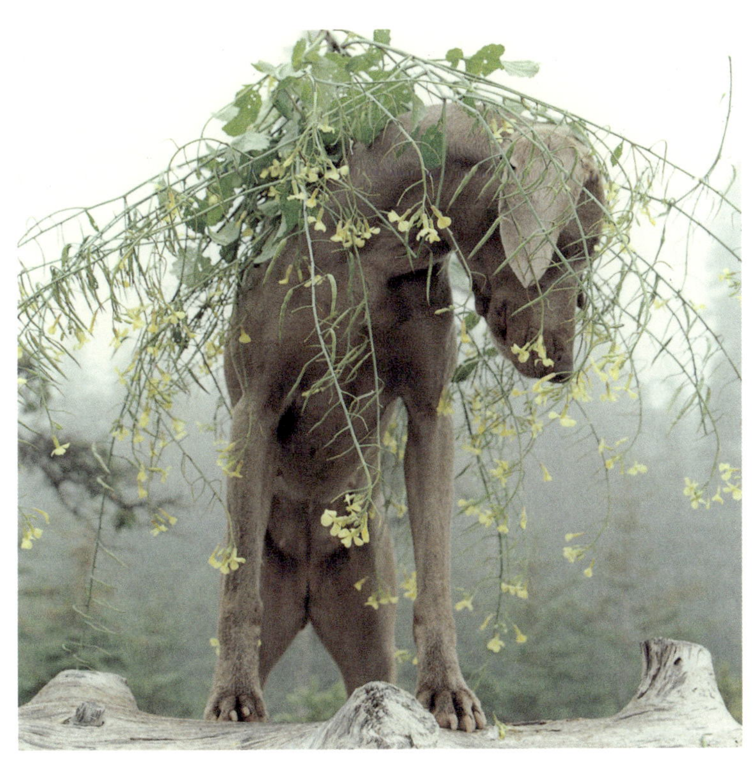

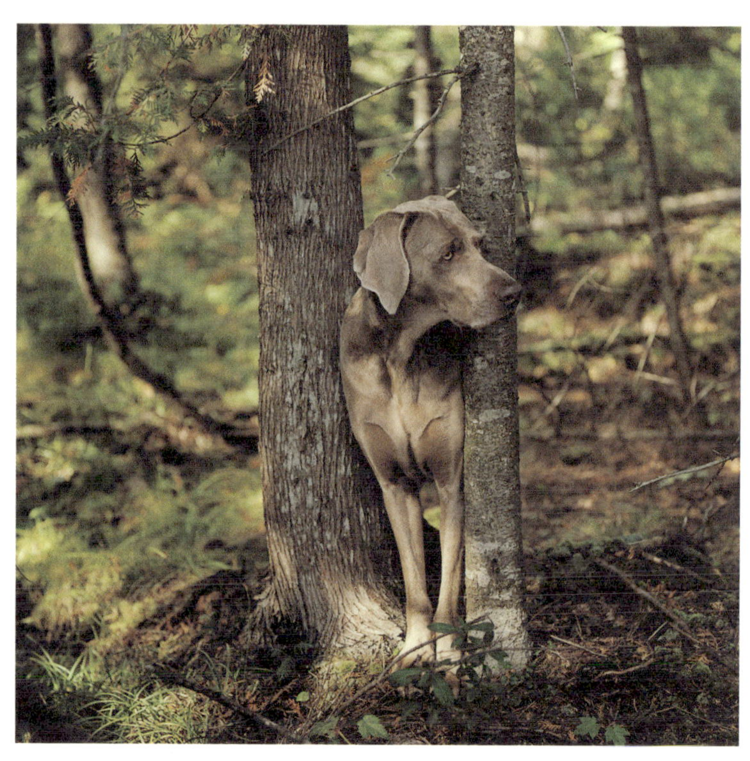

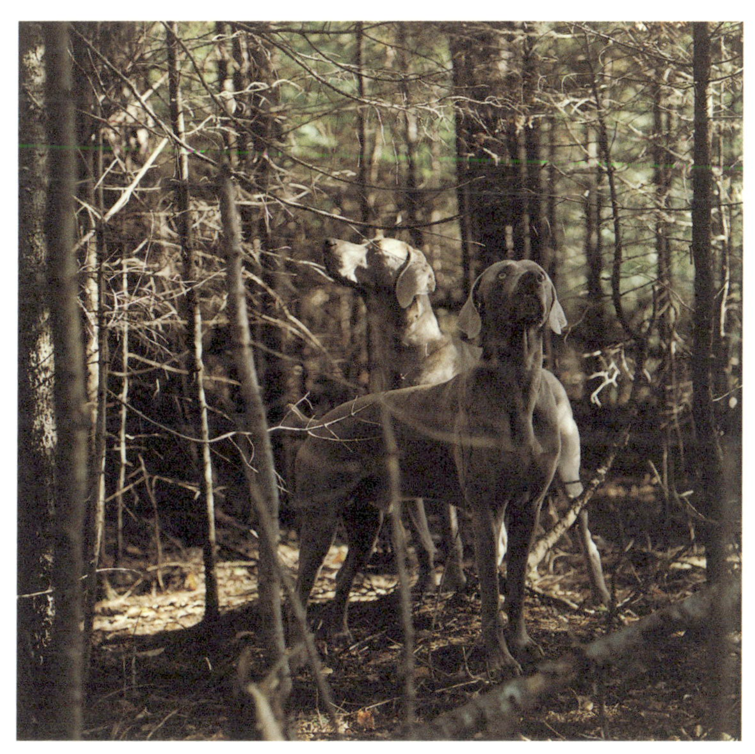

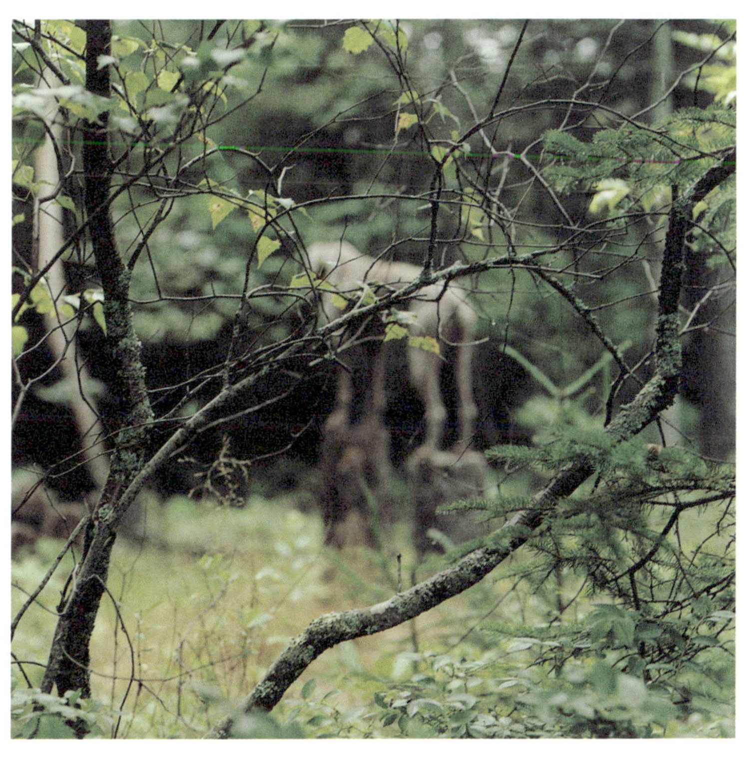

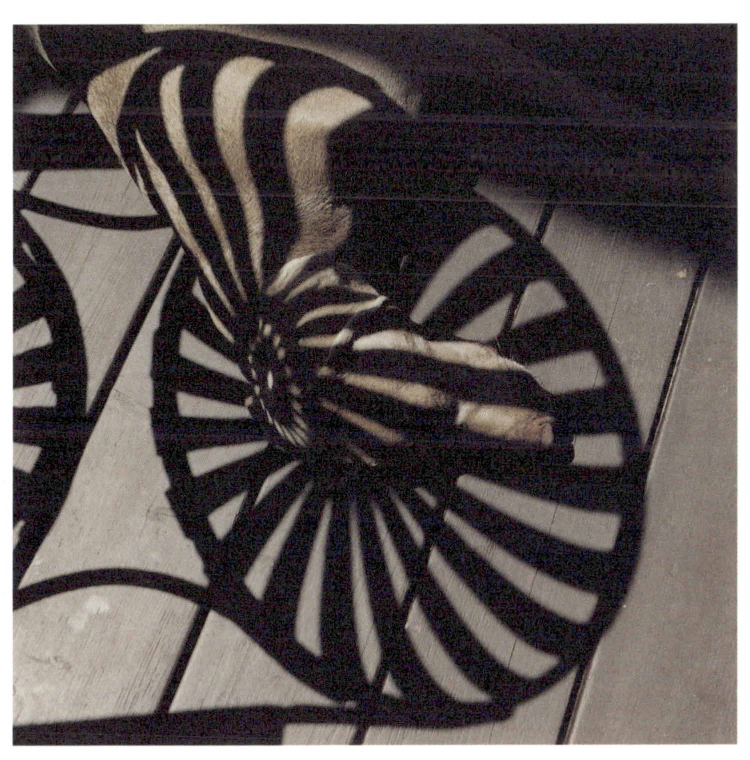

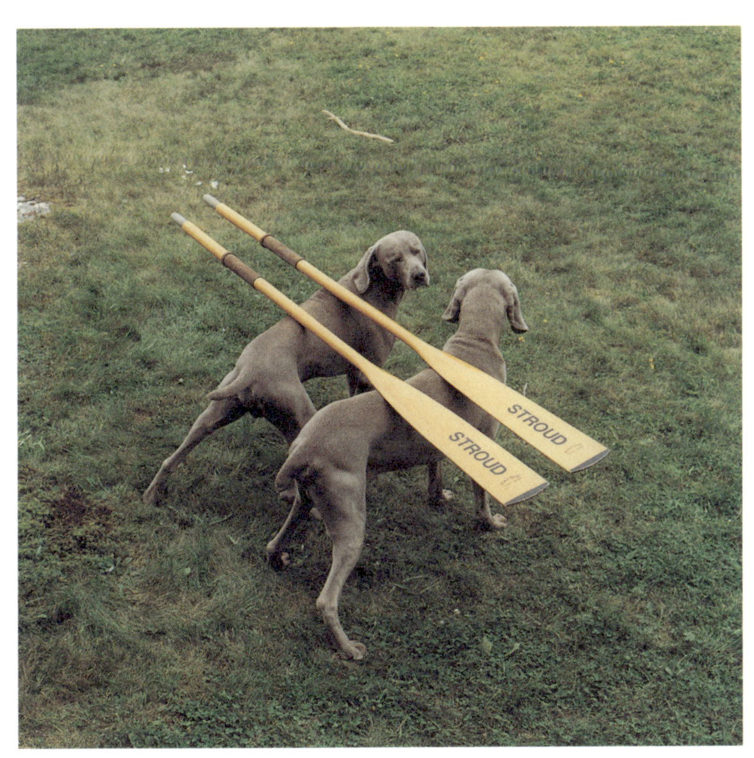
STROUD
STROUD

Biography

William Wegman was born in 1943 in Holyoke, Massachusetts. He received a B.F.A. in painting from the Massachusetts College of Art, Boston in 1965 and an M.F.A. in painting from the University of Illinois, Champagne-Urbana in 1967. From 1968 to 1970 he taught at the University of Wisconsin. In the fall of 1970 he moved to Southern California where he taught for one year at California State College, Long Beach. By the early '70s, Wegman's work was being exhibited in museums and galleries internationally. In addition to solo shows with Sonnabend Gallery in Paris and New York, Situation Gallery in London, and Konrad Fisher Gallery in Dusseldorf, his work was included in such seminal exhibitions as "When Attitudes Become Form" and "Documenta V," and regularly featured in *Interfunktionen*, *Artforum*, and *Avalanche.*

While he was in Long Beach, Wegman got his dog, Man Ray, with whom he began a long and fruitful collaboration. Man Ray, known in the art world and beyond for his endearing deadpan presence, became a central figure in Wegman's photographs and videotapes. In 1981, Man Ray died. It was not until 1986 that Wegman got a new dog, Fay Ray, and another collaboration began, marked by Wegman's extensive use of the Polaroid 20 x 24 camera. With the birth of Fay's litter in 1989, Wegman's subjects grew to include Fay's offspring—Battina, Crooky, and Chundo—and later, their offspring: Battina's son Chip in 1995, Chip's son Bobbin in 1999, and Candy and Bobbin's daughter Penny in 2004. Out of Wegman's involvement with this cast of characters grew a series of children's books inspired by the dogs' acting abilities: *Cinderella*, *Little Red Riding Hood*, *ABC*, *Mother Goose*, *Farm Days*, *My Town*, *Surprise Party*, and *Chip Wants a Dog*. Wegman has also published a number of books for adults, including *Man's Best Friend*, *Fashion Photographs*, and *William Wegman 20 x 24, Fay*, and The New York Times Bestseller *Puppies.*

Wegman has created film and video works for *Saturday Night Live* and Nickelodeon, and his video segments for Sesame Street have appeared regularly since 1989. His videos include *Alphabet Soup, Fay's Twelve Days of Christmas,* and *Mother Goose.* In 1995, Wegman's film *The Hardly Boys* was screened at the Sundance Film Festival. After a twenty-year hiatus, Wegman returned to the format of his video work from the '70s producing two new series of video works in 1998 and 1999. A collection of selected video works from 1970–99 was recently released on DVD by Artpix.

Retrospectives of Wegman's work include "Wegman's World," which opened at the Walker Art Center, Minneapolis in 1981 and toured the United States; and "William Wegman: Paintings, Drawings, Photographs, Videotapes," which opened at the Kunstmuseum, Lucerne in 1990 and traveled to venues in Europe and the United States, including the Pompidou Center, Paris, and The Whitney Museum of American Art, New York. Recent exhibitions include retrospectives in Sweden, Japan, Korea, and Spain. In 2006 the exhibition "Funney/Strange" opened at the Brooklyn Museum of Art (with a catalogue published by Yale University) and made its final stop at the Wexner Center for the Arts, Columbus, in the fall of 2007.

William Wegman lives in New York and Maine where he continues to make videos, take photographs, and make drawings and paintings.

All works are Chromogenic prints, 14 x 11 inches (35.56 x 27.94 cm), edition of twelve, and collection of the artist

The Acadia Summer Arts Program

The Acadia Summer Arts Program—commonly referred to as A.S.A.P., Kippy's Kamp, and Kamp Kippy—is an internationally known summer artist residency, located in the breathtaking Acadia National Park on Mount Desert Island, Maine. Since 1993, the program has furnished invitees with the time, space, and resources to rejuvenate their creative practices. Each year, A.S.A.P. convenes an impressive array of artists and arts professionals including museum directors, curators, architects, painters, sculptors, filmmakers, musicians, poets, dancers, and historians. The island is dotted with A.S.A.P.'s private cottages, which guests are free to use as either peaceful work space or for simple rest and relaxation. Most of the guests' time is unstructured, but the program provides weekly communal activities—dinners, guest lectures, and boat excursions to the surrounding islands—and annual public events—exhibitions, film screenings, dance performances, and concerts.

Marion "Kippy" Boulton Stroud, A.S.A.P.'s founder, has had a lifelong passion for supporting and facilitating artistic production. In 1977, she founded the Fabric Workshop and Museum in Philadelphia, where she currently serves as Artistic Director. Having spent summers on Mount Desert Island since childhood, Kippy wanted to share the beautiful Maine landscape with her friends and colleagues. Beginning as a small gathering in Kippy's coastal home, Shore Cottage, the program has blossomed into a summer-long influx of over three hundred guests each year. Consequently, the physical space has eveolved into a complex of studios, offices, and lecture facilities designed by the late Steve Izenour of Venturi, Scott Brown and Associates. Despite this growth, the intimate, familial quality of A.S.A.P. remains intact.